Presented To:

Name _____

Club _____

Date _____

Club Board
Members Guide

How To Become
an Effective Member
of Your Club Board

John L. Carroll, Esq.

Pineapple Press, Inc.
Sarasota, Florida

Inquiries should be addressed to:

Pineapple Press, Inc.
P.O. Box 3889
Sarasota, Florida 34230

www.pineapplepress.com

Library of Congress Cataloging-in-Publication Data

Carroll, John L.,
    Club board members guide : how to become an effective member of your club board / John L. Carroll.— 1st ed.
        p.   cm.
    Includes index.
    ISBN 1-56164-244-4 (pbk. : alk. paper)
    1. Clubs. 2. Boards of directors. I. Title.

HS2519 .C37 2001
367'.068'4—dc21

                                                        2001036846

First Edition
10 9 8 7 6 5 4 3 2 1

Design by Shé Sicks
Printed in the United States of America

Table of Contents

Acknowledgments

Much of what is written here comes from my years of service on many boards and as president of most of them. Each experience added to my appreciation and understanding of the work of boards. I am grateful to all those with whom I served for providing me the insights that make up the backbone of this book.

Thanks to William McMahon of the McMahon Group, Eldon Miller of the *Private Club Advisor*, attorneys Malcolm Pitchford and William O'Connor, and Jonny Cortizo of the Auckland Club of New Zealand for their very helpful suggestions. Thanks also to the many club general managers who provided valuable comments.

Thanks to Tom Finan of Finan Publishing and *Club Management* magazine, and to Hugh Jones and Mary Barnes Embody of the National Club Association for their editing comments. Special thanks to my editor, William Hutchinson, who caught my vision and gave me voice.

In addition, I wish to thank my family for their patience, their editorial skills, and their spirited comments; Joe Sandford for his insightful suggestions; Jackson Bonney and Doug Rogers for their review; and Woody Wardlow, who is always able to spot a missing comma.

Finally, a lifetime of thanks to my wife, Patricia, who, with our six children, gave us a club of our own.

Author's Note: Female readers may take issue with my use of the masculine pronoun throughout these pages. I don't blame them. But anyone who has ever tried to read a gender-neutral sentence, let alone write one, knows how convoluted language can become in the interest of cultural equality. I tried several ways to introduce a balance of female pronouns, but the result was always cumbersome. So I went with "he/him/his"—at least this time.

The increasing participation of women at all levels of club governance is one of the most significant changes I have witnessed in a lifetime of board service. Perhaps by the next edition of this book, women will have become so involved in club affairs that I'll be able to use "she/her/hers."

Introduction

*From how to keep minutes, to when to adjourn a meeting, to what
kinds of records to keep, to where to look for help when something
(anything) goes wrong—if it has to do with your service on the
board, you'll find it in this book.*

The Human Factor

Welcome to the inner circle of board membership. If your term of service
is anything like my own years on various boards of private and public
clubs, you have an invigorating experience ahead of you—and a uniquely
gratifying one.

Issues of membership, money, and maintenance aside, serving on a
club board means dealing with people—not only the club's general membership, but especially the co-directors with whom you share the responsibilities of governance.

Like any exercise in human dynamics, board service is often challeng-
ing, sometimes frustrating, occasionally aggravating, but rarely dull. The
essential give-and-take of the group process will expand your own thinking and add to your knowledge of the world. Board service builds character, you might say.

You can also say that it's fun—or should be—because a board that
doesn't laugh together doesn't promise much in the way of effective leadership. A good board, an effective board, is one that enjoys its work.

And work it is—make no mistake. As I calculate in Chapter 2, board
service requires a commitment of at least eight to twelve hours a month.
And that's if you're a fast reader who can zip through all the minutes,
committee reports, and budget summaries you will be expected to read
regularly.

In return for your time, you will be rewarded in currency of various
forms. At the very least, you will extend your network of social and business connections. If you're as lucky as I have been, you will forge new
friendships that will endure far beyond your term on the board. At most,
you will know the profound satisfaction that comes only from "service"
in its truest sense—from working for something outside yourself.

How To . . .

If you had a childhood like mine in the Midwest, you may remember setting up your first club in a backyard treehouse somewhere, and then arguing over how to run it. Who would be allowed to join? Would there be dues? Meetings? Who was going to collect those dues and run those meetings? And just whose job was it, anyway, to fix that big crack in the roof?

Eventually, somebody—probably the kid who later went to law school—suggested that maybe it would be a good idea to write down a few rules. Officers were elected. Bylaws (of a sort) were drafted, direct and to the point: "No girls allowed," in my case; maybe "No boys allowed" in yours.

Many summers later, I served on the board of a club with a $12-million facility on 360 acres of prime Florida real estate. But running that place was, in some ways, not so different. We "debated" instead of arguing, but the subjects remained pretty much the same: dues and meetings and fixing the roof. And the legal minds in our group still drove everybody crazy with their insistence on writing down every little thing.

I was that budding lawyer in my treehouse club (and became a real lawyer fifteen years after that) so, lawyer-like, what I've set out to do in these pages is precisely to write down every little thing from how to keep minutes, to when to adjourn a meeting, to what kinds of records to keep, to where to look for help when something (anything) goes wrong. If it has to do with your service on the board, you'll find it here: What should a club look for in its board members? What should a board do, what must it do, and how should it know when to keep its hands off? What's the best way to go about electing a chairman? How can board members help keep meetings on track and fully engaged? What should be in the minutes—and what should not? What can you do if a board member is more interested in being heard than in taking action?

Along the way, we'll also talk about the big things, from dealing with bylaws to terminating a general manager to creating a marketing plan and a club mission statement. We'll talk about ethics, taxes, disciplinary hearings, mediation, media relations, and—because that's what lawyers do—we'll talk about the law.

Be Prepared

While most of your time will be taken up by such matters as greens fees, dues, budgets, and membership, board service in the twenty-first century can also mean dealing with tricky questions of discrimination ("No girls allowed," indeed), sexual harassment, and environmental protection. As a board member, you will be called upon to authorize the expenditure of large sums of money. You will be entrusted with the care and maintenance of valuable real property, and with the protection of your club against liability in a litigious world.

Even if you are unlikely to face any of the more explosive problems mentioned within these pages, serving on a club board is serious business. The lawyer in me advises that it is always best to be prepared. As an experienced board member, I know that you will be more effective at your job if you fully understand the obligations and liabilities involved. The more you know about the procedures of board membership, the more tools you will have at your disposal for dealing with problems, great and small, when they do arise.

My goal here is not to burden but to free you. With a basic understanding of the mechanics of board service, you can turn your full attention to the betterment of your club and the satisfaction of its membership. From the knowledge of what is flows the imagination of what might be.

How to Read This Book

Few readers will read this book from cover to cover. Many will use it as a source book. With the exception of Chapters 12 and 13, which discuss terminating and replacing a general manager, the material is applicable to all readers who are (or are about to be) on a club board.

Chapter 1 looks at the history of private clubs from the late 1700s to the present. Chapter 2 explores how elections are held and how you can secure a spot on the board. Chapter 3 gives some insight into what you can expect as a board member. Chapter 4 sets the limitations of board action and the legal responsibilities of board members. Chapter 5 spells out the role of the club's bylaws. Chapter 6 deals with board leadership: what to look for in a good leader and how to deal with a bad one. Chapter 7 explores the dynamics of the board meeting itself. Chapter 8 stresses the importance of keeping accurate records. Chapter 9 deals with the financial aspects of club administration, including taxes and annual audits. Chapter 10 shows you how to handle the ever-present problem of complaints by and about members, employees, and others. Chapter 11 focuses on the role and evaluation of the general manager. Chapters 12 and 13 deal with terminating and hiring a general manager. Chapter 14 talks about how to secure member feedback. Chapter 15 stresses the need to plan for the future of your club. Chapter 16 discusses the various ways to communicate with your membership and the media as well as ways to handle a public relations crisis. The appendix is a complete set of bylaws for an equity club. Worth a look is the new approach to member discipline in Article IX.

So congratulations. Good luck. Have fun. And, now, let's come to order.

▲   Part One   ▲

What Have You Gotten

Yourself Into?

How the Modern Club
Board Got That Way

The earliest club boards typically consisted of charter members and/or those members with a financial interest in the organization, such as the partners in the land syndicates that built many of the early private clubs here and abroad.

British Beginnings

During the middle of the eighteenth century, roughly a century after Cervantes first noted that "birds of a feather flock together," a group of affluent English merchants and landowners took to flocking together from time to time at a London public house called Almack's. Englishmen of privilege did not (as a rule) patronize pubs, which were places for workingmen to do their drinking without offending the sensibilities of the higher orders, who usually did their drinking at home. But Almack's quickly became known as a haven for men of title and position. They could relax there, let down their powdered hair, and enjoy the thrill of slumming, elbow-to-elbow, with dockworkers and hack drivers and gamekeepers. Well, not elbow-to-elbow exactly: Edward Boodle, the general manager, took care to shield his special customers from the rabble in a private salon safely distant from the main bar.

In time, these pub evenings became so popular that the crowds of gentlemen they attracted could not be contained in a back room. Beginning in 1762, Almack's was closed for one night every fortnight for the exclusive use of these interlopers, who formalized themselves as a chartered club they named "Boodle's," after the helpful proprietor.

Boodle's is considered the precursor of the modern club. Unlike older London clubs such as White's, for example (founded a generation earlier for the male members of its charter families), Boodle's took in new members wholly on the basis of their compatible personalities, regardless of such traditional markers as birth or means or marriage. In other words, men got into Boodle's if the publican and his members wanted them in.

By the time of the American Revolution, London's social scene was bustling with dozens of private clubs established in the Boodle's mold. Many of them, including the prototype, quickly became far too large and prosperous to be restricted to occasional pub outings. In the auspicious year of 1776, Boodle's itself moved into its own clubhouse—a classically Georgian pile of marble and brick on St. James Street, paid for by a syndicate of members who leased the facility to the club.

Similar financing schemes produced many of the grand clubhouses that to this day contribute mightily to London's architectural character. Clubs jockeyed for distinction by building instant landmarks in the city's better neighborhoods. A club called The Travelers block-busted the venerable Pall Mall in 1831, locating itself in a pseudopalazzo that ushered in the Renaissance Revival era of architecture and design.

The splendor of their quarters suggests the elite status that private clubs came to enjoy in London society. Membership became increasingly competitive, and techniques were devised for the selection of suitable new members.

Notes James Mayo in his exhaustively researched book, *The American Country Club: Its Origins and Development* (Rutgers University Press, 1998): "In the 1820s London's Union Club and many others followed the practice of having a ballot box for each membership candidate. Each member was allowed to put either a white ball for approval or a black ball for denial into the candidate's ballot box. Thus the denial vote became popularly known as "blackballing."

Granddaddy of Them All

More than two hundred years after its establishment, Boodle's remains the archetypal London club.

With its soaring Venetian windows overlooking St. James Street, the venerable Georgian mansion designed in 1775 by John Crunden, is a well-known fixture of central London. Few non-members have ever had the opportunity to inspect its rooms. (Exceptions have been made. Queen Elizabeth, although a woman and therefore disqualified from membership, is among those who have entertained privately in the club's second-floor main room.)

Beyond the ornately formal main room, or "saloon," dominated by a dining table that seats thirty-two, Boodle's seems surprisingly cozy. The morning room, with its deeply upholstered, red-leather furnishings, appears as a comfortably clubby haven where one might imagine encountering Winston Churchill, grousing to himself over the pages of *The Telegraph* or *The Times*.

The organizing charter of 1763 specified that "Foreign news papers of the Hague, Amsterdam, Brussels, besides all of the London news papers, must be taken." It also mandated that "dinner is to be always upon the table at a quarter past four o'clock . . . Any member may speak for any dish cheap or dear, but he must pay for it."

Churchill became an honorary club member after World War II. Historian Edward Gibbon, economist Adam Smith, and the legendary Beau Brummell have been among the regular membership, as was Ian Fleming, who set at least one scene in Boodle's in most of his James Bond novels. ▲

Clubs in America

The French historian Alexis de Tocqueville toured the United States in 1831 and wrote *Democracy in America* in 1840. He noted that "Americans of all ages, all conditions and all dispositions constantly form associations. Feelings and opinions are recruited, the heart is enlarged and the human mind is developed by [associations created by Americans]."

In other words, as far back as the 1830s America was a country of "joiners." Clubs of every sort were created for social, religious, athletic, political, and economic reasons. Club life was an American phenomenon, more so than in England.

Old World traditions prevailed in most early American clubs. At the Philadelphia Club, established in 1834, members were even encouraged to follow the English tradition of wearing top hats, known as "tiles," while drinking at the bar. (Is this the model for those members today who insist on drinking in their golf caps?)

But American clubs differed from their English counterparts in their emphasis on food. Even with fine cognac replacing the common man's pint of bitter, most early English clubs were primarily drinking and gambling establishments. In Colonial America, where people either took their meals at home or were forced to share cutlery with their social inferiors at public taverns, it was select company over a good dinner that gentlemen craved.

The earliest private clubs in America, in fact, were probably informal groups of gourmands who periodically took over one or another tavern kitchen and dining room for a private banquet. In the early 1700s, a full century before English-style men's clubs first appeared on these shores, the South River Club of Annapolis, Maryland, was gathering in its own rough facility for regular meals.

Perhaps because of the intimacy of breaking bread together, early American club members expected facilities that were far more homelike than what the British required. While the typical English private club would have an easy-chaired library and one or two sleeping rooms for members who might overindulge, it was the bar that dominated both the space and the proceedings. Prestigious American clubs, on the other hand, typically offered a choice of parlors and sitting areas, large dining rooms, and private salons, as well

Clubs to Every Purpose

True to the diverse backgrounds of the citizens of and immigrants to the new country, American clubs tended to come in a lot more varieties than their English cousins.

By the great glory days of the Gilded Age, America's cities boasted distinguished private clubs exclusively for Jews (New York's Harmonie Club, followed by Chicago's Standard Club in 1869); blacks (Washington D.C.'s Manhattan Club, established in the 1880s); arts patrons (New York's Lotus Club, established in 1870); Dutchmen (the Knickerbocker Club in New York, founded in 1871); fishermen (the Brook Club, founded in 1902); big-game hunters (the Explorer's Club, established in 1905); and women (the Athenaeum Club in Milwaukee, built in 1887). ▲

as the essential bar. Many occupied space in converted mansions, such as the Chicago Club, founded in 1869 in the former Farnam mansion on Michigan Avenue. Several functioned as hotels, maintaining dozens of guestrooms for members, and keeping full-time domestic staffs both upstairs and down.

Origins of the Modern Country Club

Some of the earliest private clubs in America and England were primarily recreational in nature. There were yacht clubs on both sides of the Atlantic as early as 1800, and Virginia's first hunt club took root while America was still a British colony. But it wasn't until the late 1870s that social clubs commonly had the space or the inclination to provide their members with facilities for exercise or sport.

The latter years of the nineteenth century saw the rapid proliferation on the American city club scene of such amenities as exercise rooms, squash courts, swimming pools, even running tracks and tennis courts. In part, these facilities were added for competitive reasons. Major U.S. cities were by this time awash in clubs of all size

> The earliest club boards typically consisted of charter members and/or those members with a financial interest in the organization.

and description, many of them heavily mortgaged and thus financially dependent upon the steady growth of membership fees.

Also, America was by then becoming preoccupied with physical fitness. Previously content to spend their club time over brandy and cigars, the wealthy elite now sought to find amusements that fostered good health and, therefore, long life (thus to have more years left to enjoy brandy and cigars). Spas and resorts became hugely popular in the late nineteenth century, as the affluent took to the countryside in search of fresh air and mineral springs.

In 1878, a Boston lawyer named Frederick Prince sought to marry the resort with the city club on a two-hundred-acre tract of land eight miles north of Boston. Prince built tennis courts, a cricket field, and a clubhouse with bedrooms for weekend guests, then solicited memberships from 150 or so members of Boston's most prestigious city clubs.

Prince called his establishment the Myopia Hunt Club, which turned out to be appropriate, because he shortsightedly failed to recognize that eight miles was still a long way to travel in 1878. Soon, a group of the club's own members established a renegade operation four miles closer to Boston. The Country Club at Clyde Park in Brookline, founded in 1882, became an immediate success. The Myopia Hunt Club thrives yet today in Hamilton, Massachusetts.

As quoted in James Mayo's *The American Country Club*, the Brookline club's membership solicitation letter served to define what we might today call the club's mission: "The general idea is to have a comfortable clubhouse for the use of members with their families, a simple restaurant, bed-rooms, bowling-alley, lawn-tennis grounds, etc; also to have race-meetings and, occasionally, music in the afternoons . . ."

No matter that it distinguished between "members," all of whom were male, and "their families," the Brookline group established the prototype of the country club as a mixed-gender, multi-generational gathering place. Slowly but steadily, other such clubs took shape around the country, among them the St. Andrews Club of Yonkers, New York, which opened in 1888 with the revolutionary amenity of a six-hole course for the playing of a game called golf.

Enter Golf

Regardless of its Scottish ancestry, golf was a pastime seemingly made for America at the turn of the twentieth century. Anybody could play it, for one thing, and the risks of physical danger in doing so were minimal, at most. Golf was not identifiably a game for vigorous young people nor did it require years of training (like, say, horseback riding) nor extraordinary investment (like yachting).

Golf was competitive and yet, because it was played in groups, the game fostered fellowship. And golf was new to America. Because the pastime was not bound to traditional associations of old-money privilege—as was polo, for example—it was especially appealing to an emerging class of affluent men.

Golf was first played sometime early in the fifteenth century. King James I is believed to have introduced the game to London around 1608. The first golf club in the modern mold was the Royal and Ancient Golf Club of St. Andrew's, Scotland, established in 1754. Popularly called the R&A, St. Andrew's became the governing body for golf throughout the Commonwealth and beyond. Today, the international rules of golf are set jointly by the United States Golf Association and the R&A.

The first formal golf course in America was a three-hole course built in 1885 by a wealthy gamesman in Foxburg, Pennsylvania, for his own use. Just three years later, however, St. Andrews Golf Club in Yonkers, New York, became the first private club to build a golf course for the use of its membership. It began with three holes at first. Later, three more were carved into an adjacent cow pasture.

The founders of the American St. Andrews were both Scots—Robert Lockhart and John Reid, the latter dubbed the "father" of American golf. It was Reid who pushed the game—then played with three woods, three irons, and "gutta-percha" balls made from plant materials imported from Malaysia.

Over the next fifteen years, more than one thousand such clubs were established in the United States, including the elegant

Shinnecock Hills Golf Club in Southampton, New York (1891), which featured an unheard-of twelve holes. The Chicago Golf Club (actually located in Wheaton, Illinois, and founded in 1892) for a while standardized the nine-hole course as the national norm.

The turn of the twentieth century was a busy time for the founding of golf clubs throughout America, and many of these clubs are still active and flourishing today (such as my old club, the Evansville [Indiana] Country Club, which celebrated its 100th Anniversary in 2000).

In 1894, the United States Golf Association (USGA) was founded to formulate a standard set of rules for the game. (Among these was the handicapping system that makes modern golf the most democratic of sports.) Only seven years later, in 1901, *Harper's Weekly* took note of the golfing craze and reported that every state in the union had at least one such club.

Early Methods of Member Selection

Blackballing was one of the traditions that came across the Atlantic as private clubs took root on these shores in the century after the Revolution. At the Somerset Club in Boston, founded in 1829, it took three black marbles to reject a new member. At the Union Club in New York, founded the same year, it took five. (A quarter-century later, the Union Club's periodic membership votes, and the names of those blackballed, were of such interest as to be reported in the pages of *The New York Times*.)

More commonly, though, American private clubs assigned to a board of governors the task of judging—in secret—an applicant's suitability for membership. These original boards inevitably took on the responsibilities of assessing and collecting dues and fees from the membership. In time, their job expanded further to include the duty of disseminating information on matters of common interest to the members—an increase in dues and fees, for example, or a special assessment intended to finance some improvement or increases in services.

The earliest club boards typically consisted of charter members and/or those members with a financial interest in the organization, such as the partners in the land syndicates that built many of the early private clubs in this country and abroad.

Early boards were usually "self-perpetuating" in that the board itself was allowed to fill vacancies among its group. But self-perpetuating boards created traditions of dynastic control at odds with the more democratic nature of private clubs in America. Here, rank-and-file members sought to increase their voice in club affairs by insisting that board members be selected in the usual democratic way: a general election.

The sort of Americans who were in a position to join clubs in the nineteenth century believed that there certainly was such a thing as too much democracy, however. Thus was born the tradition of the nominating committee, whose responsibility it was to propose pre-screened candidates for the board. ▲

Becoming a Board Member: Nominations and Elections

Assembling a good slate of board candidates is like creating a mosaic, each piece fitting neatly with the next—no overlaps and no gaps.

Nominating Committees

Early on, nominating committees were often drawn entirely from the governing boards themselves, but this practice largely disappeared as club memberships recognized that this, too, was a tool of self-perpetuation. Today, most nominating committees are composed predominantly of non-board members, appointed by the club president with the approval of the club board.

Selection of a committee to propose members for the board is tricky. Nominators should be among the ablest of club members—those most familiar with club policy and traditions, and most committed to club service. They should be, in other words, first-rate candidates for positions on the board. But in most cases, club bylaws bar the nominating committee from nominating one of its own.

Some clubs weight the nominating committee heavily with ex-members of the board. Many make it a point to have one or more past presidents on the committee. These are both excellent ways of supplementing a nominating committee, but it is important that the committee be as broadly based as possible.

At best, the committee should be composed of people from different corners of the club, representing variations in age, gender, and interests yet sharing an appreciation for the unique traditions and character of the club.

Selecting the Best Candidates

In considering candidates for board seats, the nominating committee will naturally focus first on club members who have actively demonstrated their interest in club service, perhaps through membership on committees. But many worthy candidates (in my experience, oftentimes women) are too shy or modest to bring themselves forward. A special effort should be made to recruit qualified women as nominees, as they bring a unique perspective to the board. The nominating committee should begin its work with a careful analysis of the *full* membership for possible nominees.

Some people can be excluded quickly from substantive consideration—those who have been direct about not wanting to be considered for positions on the board, for example, or those who are well known to lack the time required or who live too far away to attend meetings.

The nominating committee may also exclude some members for more subjective reasons. Opposing opinions are important components of any successful board, but it is wise for the nominating committee to avoid those members who obviously enjoy conflict more than resolution, those who respect no opinions but their own, and those who are not open to fair discussion. It is a mistake to nominate a vocal dissident in the hopes of taming him. He is not likely to change and if he is elected, the board could have a troublemaker on its hands.

Candidates who make the nominating committee's first cut should be considered as potential board members according to the following criteria:

- **Is this the sort of person who can be trusted to "do the right thing" for the institution of the club, without regard to external pressures or self-interest?** Is the candidate a fair person, deliberative but not ponderous, able to grasp opposing points of view and make a reasoned choice?

- **Does the candidate have the time to be a good board member?** Typically, a club board member can expect to attend one board meeting a month, each lasting from two to three hours, with the occasional five-hour marathon. Beyond regular meetings, there may be one or two "special sessions" a year, each lasting an hour or so. Every meeting requires homework (reading committee reports, financial statements, and proposals for board action), which might take several hours. Committee service will add another two or three hours a month—much more for the chairman and those committees whose mission is particularly sensitive (grounds, house, and membership, for example). You will find that members often feel free to telephone board members at home in order to discuss one or another "urgent" piece of business. All in all, it takes an average of about eight to twelve hours a month.

- **Has the candidate clearly demonstrated the ability to work with others?** A typical board of directors will meld the energies and talents of many different kinds of people—those who see the forest, those who see the trees, those who count the bears. A good candidate for board membership is the individual who can listen with respect to all points of view.

- **Has the candidate been a member long enough to understand and appreciate the club's traditions and mission?** Be wary of the revolutionary who favors change for change's sake and lacks any real appreciation for the club as it is.

- **Does the candidate possess leadership skills?** Optimism, confidence, integrity, decisiveness, persuasive skills of articulation: these are qualities that a nominating committee should look for in any candidate for the board.

- **Can the candidate accept criticism?** A volatile person who raises his voice and turns red in a locker-room discussion of golf scores is probably going to behave the same way at a board meeting. Similarly, it is a good idea to avoid those candidates whose response to conflict is to walk away from it. A board cannot function well if one of its members daintily absents himself from the room if and when things get heated. (The president of one board on which I served actually did this regularly, but that's another story.)

- **Is the candidate a well-rounded person?** The tennis-court ace who sees the world in terms of match points may have the admiration of the club membership but may not be the best candidate for board service. Wisdom and prudence, qualities required of an effective board member, are most likely found in an individual whose interests include history, world affairs, human psychology, and the countless idiosyncrasies of group dynamics.
- **Is the candidate well liked and respected by fellow club members?** Any board election—like it or not, an election of any kind—is in part a popularity contest. A gifted executive with superior skills might seem a great addition to the board, but if he rubs too many members the wrong way, they're not going to be happy with the nominating committee's choice.
- **Finally, each candidate for the board should be considered according to the special skills or areas of expertise he brings to the table.** Does the candidate have a special talent that the board needs, such as legal, accounting, engineering, communications, or management? Assembling a good slate of board candidates is like creating a mosaic, with each piece fitting neatly to the next—no overlaps and no gaps.

The Case Against Open Elections

Not all of the board candidates selected by the nominating committee will agree to serve. The committee should prepare a preliminary roster that identifies twice as many candidates as there are openings on the board. This list should be kept strictly confidential as a committee instrument; no one wants to know that he is the committee's second choice for a seat.

From its preliminary list, the committee assembles a final slate of board candidates. Ideally, the number of names proposed will equal the number of seats available.

> If the nominating committee has done its job well, the slate of candidates it presents will reflect the diversity of personalities, interests, and opinions that characterizes any vital, flourishing private club.

In order to give the membership greater choice in the selection of their governors, many clubs have opened up board elections to the general membership by proposing candidates from which the membership may choose its favorites. However well-intentioned, open elections can create more problems than they are worth. For one thing, you're opening yourself up to an election-by-crapshoot. When the general membership votes, good golf scores and an affable nature often count for more than administrative skills and club vision.

Secondly, many qualified candidates will choose not to stand for an open election to avoid the possible embarrassment of defeat. (The same problem has been faced by the judiciary in this country, where many well-qualified lawyers are unwilling to "run" for a judgeship.)

Says Frank Vain, president of the McMahon Group, a club-consulting firm: "It is difficult to find qualified people today who will put in the time and energy necessary to serve on a club board. If you are going to then require that this successful member with the skills and vision necessary to help the club must go through an open election, you probably just cut the slim pool of candidates by another half to two-thirds."

If the nominating committee has done its job well, however, the slate of candidates it presents will reflect the diversity of personalities, interests, and opinions that characterizes any vital, flourishing private club.

In one club of my acquaintance, the nominating committee received ten resumés for three openings on the board. In the name of democracy, the committee nominated all ten. Result: One candidate was elected by a small minority of members.

It is the job of the nominating committee to convince the general membership of the wisdom of its choices. Even when the balloting itself is no more than a formality, members need to feel personally certain that their interests are being represented with competence and fairness. "Meet the Candidates" nights and the distribution of resumés are two tried-and-true ways to familiarize the membership with the slate of candidates.

You're a Nominee—Now What?

If the number of nominees equals the number of openings, there is little for the candidate to do except be alert for nominations from the floor or by member petition. In either case there will be a contest, and you as a candidate need to be prepared.

If the club has open elections, now what? How can you get your name out so members will know to vote for you? In a way, it's the same problem every candidate for office has to deal with, whether running for the city council or for the presidency of the United States. There is a difference, though. Every private club has a tradition on how candidates are expected to act and the candidate who violates that tradition does so at great peril. Understanding the tradition of the club is to understand the way candidates have conducted themselves over the years. If a candidate ignores this tradition, the members will think he does not understand what the club is and what it stands for.

In the early campaigns for the presidency of the United States, it was considered unseemly for the candidate to do anything to promote his candidacy. Neither John Adams nor Thomas Jefferson campaigned for the office. In later years, William McKinley was elected president while sitting on his front porch in Canton, Ohio. Things have come a long way since then, but for the most part, candidates for private club boards still follow the early model by not actively seeking the office they so greatly desire.

Each club has its tradition and the astute board candidate should be aware of it. Having said that, the candidate would be foolish to sit on his front porch and hope for the best.

Most clubs send to the membership a resumé prepared by each candidate. Great care should be taken in the preparation of the resumé. What could be worse than to have a misspelling or a false claim of education, for example? Have a literate friend help with the resumé and be sure it is accurate. Be sure to include only information that is relevant to the job. Education: yes. Job experience: yes. Club activity: yes. Military experience: probably no. Religion: probably no. Number of former wives: no. Wealth: no. What talent might you bring to board service? If you are a lawyer, an accountant, a banker, a management person, an engineer, or have other talents that can serve the club, stress them in the resumé.

Within the club's tradition, there is always room for creativity. In some clubs, where the election is held at the annual meeting, signs, posters, banners, and campaign buttons are within the tradition. But for most clubs, electioneering is subtler. Here is where creativity comes in. A cocktail party for friends of the candidate may well be within the tradition. It is an expensive but effective way of motivating friends to talk up the candidacy.

The best way of being elected and staying within the club's tradition is through the "buzz." It is rare that a candidate is known by all of the members. People talk and your friends can start the buzz on your behalf.

    A. Who should I vote for? I know only one person on the list.

    B. Well, I'm voting for Jan Smith. She's got a lot of moxie and she's an accountant, something we need on the board.

What better advertisement could a candidate have?

However, the buzz can work negatively. The fact that a candidate got intoxicated and hit a bartender or is always late in paying his club bill and is regularly posted for nonpayment quickly circulates among the members and becomes negative buzz.

If skillfully composed, a mailing to the membership describing the candidate's credentials can be a powerful election device. If the mailing is by a well-known and respected member, so much the better.

Respect your club's tradition, but find creative ways to get your name and talents out and you will come home a winner. ▲

Learning the Ropes

3

In order to be effective in his or her role, the new member must first and foremost possess an understanding of the board's delegated role in the functioning of the club.

Orientation

Soon after your election, you should expect to receive from the board or from the club manager an information packet containing the following:

- The club's bylaws and rules
- Its mission statement and strategic-planning report
- A list of the club's committees and an explanation of each committee's function
- A copy of the current budget
- The latest financial statement
- The schedule of regular board meetings
- The minutes of the last board meeting

The more background material you are provided, the better—and it is a very good idea to read it all. In accepting a position on the board, you are tacitly putting your own signature to each of these documents, lending the weight of your name to each of the

> In becoming a director, you have taken on what is known as a "fiduciary position" in your club's affairs, meaning you are now legally bound to protect the organization's assets and interests as diligently as you would your own.

activities and attitudes described. You are, in effect, signing a contract with the club. (As your "attorney," I must remind you never to sign any contract you haven't read and understood.)

In becoming a director, you have taken on what is known as a "fiduciary position" in your club's affairs, meaning you are now legally bound to protect the organization's assets and interests as diligently as you would your own. Under the law, you must perform your duties in a manner that you reasonably believe to be conducive to the general good of the club.

This requires that you possess a reasonable understanding of what *constitutes* the general good of the club—which in turn means that you must possess a detailed understanding of the club's finances and operations. The effective board member will begin his term of service by learning everything useful about the organization he is now sworn to protect.

Not long after receiving your information packet, you should expect to meet with the club president and general manager for a familiarization tour of the facility. This may take the form of a structured orientation session or informal walk-through. It may involve all the board newcomers at once or one at a time.

In all cases, however, this inspection should provide a chance for every new board member to become acquainted with the club's facilities, equipment, and the typical club's principal expense areas: foodservice, recreation, and administration.

Take this opportunity to introduce yourself to the chef, golf course superintendent, membership director, and office manager, each of whom has an intimate understanding of matters that may require board attention. Take your cues from the general manager, who will probably be leading your tour, but don't be afraid to ask questions of your own. Be careful not to make a pest of yourself. This is no time to suggest that the chef's Bordelaise sauce lacks bounce. If you want to suggest a new invoice system to the office manager, bring it up on another occasion. Say hello and then let *them* talk.

Observe the general manager as well. You've no doubt already formed some opinion of him through your dealings as a rank-and-file member. Now, though, you must consider the GM as a fellow member of your club's administrative team. Solicit his opinions on the club's mission and long-range plans, and encourage frank discussion of any major problems he feels the club may be facing. This is a good time to observe whether the manager seems to have a long-range vision for the club.

What You Need to Know

Whether through a formal orientation or a less-structured approach, the new member should begin his term of service with a fairly comprehensive understanding of the following:

- **The club's bylaws**. These make up the road map by which your club is governed. Crafted, approved, and amended by the full membership, they define what the board can do on its own (such as raising dues) and what it can do only with the expressed consent of the membership (e.g., levying a special assessment).
- **And its rules**. Rules are specific regulations of conduct and behavior. Usually, the board has the authority to change or modify the rules without member approval. It is a board member's legal obligation to see to it that the rules are followed, whether that means a gentle admonition to an out-of-bounds smoker or a pointed reprimand to a party animal serenading in the members' bar.
- **The club's history**. When was it founded, by whom, and for what purpose? How has its mission changed over time? I admit to my strong prejudice here: I do not believe that any person can effectively govern any institution without knowledge of the traditions that originally shaped it and an understanding of the deliberations through which it has evolved.
- **The financial profile**. At a minimum, prepare yourself for board service by becoming conversant with the annual bud-

get (broken down month-by-month) and the current financial statement.

- *The first thing to examine is whether the club's financial statements have been professionally prepared, audited, and certified.* Can you understand them? Are they straightforward in their presentation of information? You should be able to tell at a glance whether the club is solvent and able to meet its obligations. And you should be able to perceive some sense of where the club is headed financially.

- *Is the budget being followed?* Are any disturbing long-term trends apparent—declines in membership rolls, for example, or escalating food costs in the kitchen? How has the club structured its payment of long-term debt? Read the footnotes of the annual, audited financial statements for mentions of pending tax audits or litigation or changes in accounting procedure that might have a negative impact on the balance sheet. (More on this in Chapter Nine.)

- *What happens to initiation fees?* Are they set aside in a fund earmarked for special projects—the Baltimore Country Club, for example, devotes initiation fees to the capital improvement fund—or do they get lumped into operating revenues with day-to-day dues and charges?

- *What method of accounting does the club employ?* If it's a simple cash method, records will show only completed transactions: money in and money out. In the more sophisticated and more commonly used accrual method, income and expenses are recorded as they are incurred, as accounts receivable and accounts payable.

- **The division of responsibility.** In order to be effective in his role, the new member must possess an understanding of the board's delegated role in the functioning of the club. He must understand the board's relationship not only to the general manager, but also to the committees of the club.

Subject to the powers expressly assigned to the membership in the bylaws, the board has the ultimate authority in fulfilling the mission of the club. Like the federal government of the United States, or the governments of any of its component states, the board exercises its authority in three ways:

- *Legislative Power*: by establishing the mission of the club and creating the policies that guide its day-to-day operation
- *Executive Power*: by selecting the general manager, approving the annual budget, setting the dues, approving all major expenditures, and generally overseeing all operations of the club
- *Judicial Power*: by acting as the final, internal court of appeal in matters pertaining to personnel, membership, and discipline

Ultimately, though, members of the board of directors exercise their authority through *Collective Power*. If a board is to function properly, individual personalities must be blended; even passionately held minority viewpoints must eventually give way to the will of the majority. The board is corporate; it acts on the basis of group discussion.

In preparing for your first board meeting, keep in mind the words of British mathematician and philosopher Alfred North Whitehead, who said, "No member of a crew is praised for the rugged individuality of his rowing."

What the Board Does

The specific responsibilities of the board at your club may vary but should include the following:

- Setting the club's mission and ensuring that activities of the club are consistent with that mission
- Developing and implementing a strategic or long-range plan, and seeing to it that the plan is reviewed from time to time
- Hiring (and terminating, if necessary) the general manager and establishing the terms and conditions of his or her employment
- Reviewing the performance of the general manager at least annually, according to pre-established standards

The Board Member's Code of Ethics

As a board member of this club, I agree that I will:

- Approach all matters coming before the board with an open mind, with the intent to make the best decision for everyone involved
- Represent all members of the club and not favor those having special interests either within or outside the club
- Focus on the mission of the club and not my own personal agenda
- Consider myself a "guardian" of the club and do my best to ensure that its properties are well maintained, financially strong, and always operated in the best interests of the club and its members
- Respect and support the majority decisions of the board
- Not use the club or my services on this board for my personal gain or for the gain of those close to me
- Never exercise authority as a board member except in a meeting of the board or as delegated by the board
- Keep confidential the employee records and disciplinary matters of club members, unless the board elects to publicize the matter
- Not undermine a board decision with which I may disagree ▲

- Approving the hiring and/or firing of the professional staff
- Approving the yearly budget as prepared by the general manager and staff in conjunction with the club officers, then monitoring the budget to see that it is being properly followed
- Setting the annual dues and other charges in the manner defined in the bylaws
- Monitoring all major expenditures of the club

The Golden Mean

"The principle of the golden mean applies with striking relevance to the work of board members. It is essential that they do enough, but not too much; that they deliberate at sufficient length but not too long; that they are forceful when necessary, but quiet when they should be; that they hold fast to what they believe but are not obstinate; and that they share their knowledge, but not spout it forth at excessive length."
—From *Governing Boards* by Cyril Houle (Jossey-Bass, San Francisco, 1989).▲

- Approving the selection of the club's outside auditor and carefully reviewing the audit at year's end
- Overseeing the club's insurance coverage
- Originating all assessment requests
- Originating and approving all amendments to the club bylaws
- Setting and amending the club rules
- Defining the responsibilities of all committees and approving/appointing members of those committees
- Acting as the final arbiter in the admission of new members and in the disciplining of members
- Selecting the club president and other officers from among the membership of the board

By now, it may well have occurred to you that the modern club board member has extensive authority over club affairs. With that power comes, as always, a proportionate amount of responsibility.

Inevitably, you will find that your service on the board changes your perspective on club affairs. In a way, you cease to be a club member. A member is the octogenarian who's been part of the club for sixty years and doesn't understand why his dues should be raised to support construction of a new clubhouse he'll never live to see. A member is the man who wants to donate a new library to

> You will find that your service on the board changes your perspective on club affairs. In a way, you cease to be a club member.

the club as long as his wife can decorate it. A member is the man who thinks the general manager ought to be horsewhipped for taking rice pudding off the Sunday supper menu.

A board member must be a skilled juggler who can manage these and other (often conflicting) desires among the membership. Perhaps the first lesson the new board member must take to heart is the oldest rule by which all men of principle must live: There is no way to please all the people all the time. ▲

Legal Matters

The law requires that board decisions be made on a rational basis and exercised with due care.

Fixing the Blame

Board members share potential legal responsibility for club actions undertaken during their term of service, from the officers they elect, to the contracts they draw, to the disciplinary actions they take against individual members.

Over time, the courts have found board members responsible for such misdeeds as engaging in illegal activity, self-dealing, abetting the misdeeds of others, allowing inefficient management, authorizing the sale of club assets for less than fair value, creating unnecessary tax liabilities, approving fraudulent or misleading minutes and reports, incurring debt that the institution has no means of repaying, failing to properly monitor financial records, and, oh yes, for slandering/libeling members who have been disciplined or applicants who have been rejected for membership.

Personally, I have never suffered any legal consequences as a result of my affiliation with a board of directors. The likelihood is

> A board member's best protection is his ability to demonstrate that he has acted according to the basic precepts of sound business judgment.

slim that your term of board service will wind you up in court. But I believe in being prepared for what is at least theoretically possible, particularly since it is relatively easy for the board member to protect himself against legal action.

A board member's best protection is his ability to demonstrate that he has acted according to the basic precepts of sound business judgment. The Business Judgment Rule, as it is called in most states, requires that a board of directors act in good faith and that their conduct be lawful, reasonable, and in the legitimate furtherance of the organization's purposes.

In other words, board decisions must be made on a rational basis and exercised with due care. The law even assists in defining what is rational due care by defining three specific areas of responsibility that directors, individually or collectively, must uphold:

1. The "Duty of Diligence" means that the board member must perform his duties with the care of a reasonably prudent person in similar circumstances.

> Sounds simple enough. How diligent behavior is construed, however, may be open to interpretation. Is it diligent for the board to put off clubhouse repairs because some members feel strongly against imposing any special assessments during their term of service? The delay won't seem so diligent when the next board has to deal with the consequences of deferred maintenance—a roof that might have been patched now needing replacement, leaky plumbing that has slowly eroded the underpinnings of the entire clubhouse.

2. The "Duty of Loyalty" requires that the interests of the club always come first. No board member can take advantage of his position for personal gain. He may not secure secret profits or unfair gain at the expense of the club, nor compete with the club to its disadvantage.

The wise board member will avoid even the *appearance*

When to Call Your Lawyer

- Lawsuits: Filed or threatened, any lawsuit should be brought to your counselor's attention immediately.
- Bylaws: If there's a serious question of interpretation, leave it to your attorney, preferably in a written opinion.
- Employment Issues: Report at once any employee grievances in the areas of wage and hour disputes, sexual harassment, or employee discharge.
- Criminal Misconduct: Report possible misconduct by any employee or board member.
- Contracts: Any employment contract should be reviewed by your attorney before the club's designees have signed it. Also, run by him any contracts that obligate the club for more than one year.
- Real Estate: Consult on all matters involving buying, selling, or leasing real estate, claims of nuisance or encroachment, and anything having to do with environmental law or zoning.
- Membership: Seek a legal opinion regarding all serious disciplinary matters, admission issues, and changes in membership-class rights, including claims of discrimination based on gender.
- Insurance: Discuss with your attorney any major changes in coverage, all disputes regarding coverage, reservation of rights, and any issue regarding the club's Directors & Officers Liability (D&O) coverage.
- Governmental Notices: Bring to your attorney's attention any notice from any public agency when there exists the possibility of litigation, a public hearing, or penalties. ▲

of a conflict of interest, because nothing sets the membership's heads a-bobbin' like the suspicion that one of their own may be profiting at their expense.

3. The "Duty of Compliance" means that a board member must act at all times according to the governing laws of the community,

> It is the board's responsibility to keep reasonably abreast of all regulations that pertain to its operations.

state, and nation, and within the rules and regulations of the club itself.

Let's say the club has a house merlot that is universally enjoyed by the membership (an unlikely situation, by the way, but never mind). As a gesture of goodwill, the club decides to make the wine available by the case to the members at a modest, cost-plus profit of ten percent. This seemingly innocent plan is actually fraught with potential consequences.

The club almost certainly needs a special license to sell alcoholic beverages for consumption off the premises. Even with that license, the club may be acting *ultra vires* ("beyond the scope") by engaging in a form of commerce not designated in its own charter documents. Further, if the club is tax-exempt under Internal Revenue Code §501(c)(7), such sales could jeopardize its privileged standing with the I.R.S.

Ignorance of the law, as you may have heard, is no excuse. It is the board's responsibility to keep reasonably abreast of all regulations that pertain to its operations. Especially in the volatile fields of environmental and zoning law (where new rules seem to appear without warning overnight), the board must combine diligence with compliance in staying on top of quick changes.

If there is an attorney on the board—as there almost always is—it is a good idea to ask him to review professional journals and other publications regularly in order to remain abreast of legal developments that may have an impact on your club's business. One way of keeping on top of legal changes is by subscribing to a monthly newsletter such as *The Private Club Advisor* or by becoming a member of the National Club Association.

In one club where there was no lawyer elected to the board, the board appointed a club member lawyer as an *ex officio* (non-voting member) with authority to attend board meetings but with no power to vote. In that club, the lawyer's monthly dues were waived.

How to Hire a Lawyer

It's often handy to have a lawyer on the board, but that's not the same thing as having legal representation. In fact, conflict-of-interest issues probably would prevent an attorney who is a member of your board from acting as its legal representative. In any event, it's not a wise thing to do.

Every private club should have a lawyer, someone on whom the board can call for fully-thought-out opinions on questions of corporate law, employment law, real estate law, tax law, environmental law, and interpretations of the club bylaws.

The club's attorney does not represent the board. He represents the club as an institution, but it is the board that selects him. Or them, if you select a firm instead of an individual practitioner, which is one of the first decisions to be made.

Your club may get more personalized, special attention from the independent practitioner, that's true, but in a sticky situation you are likely to be better represented by a firm with multiple specialties. Just make sure one person within the firm is designated as your principal contact person, the one whose job it is to return your phone calls promptly and remain otherwise available.

The board should begin its search by selecting a list of three to five candidates rated "A/V" in the *Martindale-Hubbell Legal Directory* (available in most library reference rooms). The "A" represents a letter-grade assessment of legal performance; the "V", for "very good," designates the attorney's character rating by his or her own peers. Less than twenty percent of all attorneys receive the top A/V rating, so by choosing from among this select group, you know you're getting the best.

The club president (or his designee) should write to the firms selected for consideration, inviting them to submit a proposal for representation, which should include the name and qualifications of the individual within the firm who would be the club's principal contact person.

A small committee of the board might then interview the most promising of the candidates. It's always best to have this initial meeting on the lawyers' own turf so you can survey the scene with a critical eye. Is the reception area appealing and orderly? Are clients greeted in a professional fashion? Are the magazines up-to-date? (As the Shakers say, God is in the details. If you're going to have to wait fifteen minutes from time to time—which you will, I assure you—you're not going to be content with that dog-eared *Field & Stream* from 1994.)

Three members is an ideal size for this screening committee. That's enough people to break a tie but not so many as to become unwieldy—or look pretentious. It may be judicious of the board to include the club manager as one member of this group.

In any case, each member should be involved in soliciting nuts-and-bolts information, such as:

- What direct experience, if any, do the attorneys have with club affairs?
- Do they seem to grasp the special public-relations considerations involved in a club's legal profile?
- What is their fee system like, and what is their preferred method of compensation?
- Would they be amenable to accepting a small retainer, thereby ensuring that they will not represent another client whose interests are adverse to the club's? Will they accept the retainer against billings, rather than considering it a separate fee?

The committee should also be developing a subjective sense of the firm's style. Are these articulate people? Accomplished? Confident? Polished? Likable?

At the conclusion of this session, ask for references. You may have already talked to some people about the firm but it is always useful to find out what its most favored clients have to say.

Call the references and ask real questions. Some people take this step as a ceremonial formality, but the object of getting references is to solicit useful information about the firm's skill at practicing law and mode of doing business. (It is best to assign this task to a non-attorney, by the way, to avoid the complication of professional discretion.) If your state and/or local bar association has a discipline committee, it never hurts to call them as well.

When the committee has reached its decision, the designated lawyer(s) should be invited to meet with the full board and the club manager, this time at the club.

Prior to this session, the candidate should be provided copies of all relevant club documents: mission statement, bylaws, club rules and regulations, financial statements, and major contracts (including that with the club's original developer).

This is the time to negotiate fees and terms of the relationship, but don't try to haggle as if you were buying a used car. If your preferred candidate is going to cost the club more than it can legitimately afford, you have no choice but to move on to the next name on your list. Try to get your attorney to send regular monthly bills, rather than allowing billable hours to accumulate throughout the entire process of a specific action or service. Otherwise the club may be in for a big surprise.

It is not necessary to conclude this meeting with a firm offer. In fact, it would be a smart gesture of courtesy toward the general manager that he be allowed to approve the candidate before any deal is made.

The deliberative and methodical approach I have outlined here is actually the cornerstone of the "lawyerly" approach. No attorney should fault you for being thorough in your search for the right board representative. In fact, your willingness to take extra pains will send the clearest possible signal to the attorney you select that the board is well aware of its legal responsibilities.

Cover Yourself: Insurance

The board's responsibility for protecting the club's assets involves making certain that those assets are properly insured. The primary rule of thumb is: "Insure everything that you can't afford to lose."

Any new board member would be well advised to examine the club's insurance policies. Most club officers and directors do not read the fine print of an insurance policy until a major loss occurs. Sometimes a close reading turns up surprises as to what is covered and what is not. A competent insurance broker or the club's lawyer can help avoid such surprises, but someone on the board should be charged with an annual review of *all* the club's insurance. It's also wise to send the club's insurance business out for bids every three or four years.

Beyond life and health insurance for its employees, and mandatory workers' compensation insurance, what follows are the main categories of insurance required for a well-protected club:

- **General Liability Insurance** covers bodily injury and property damage, personal injury and advertising liability, medical payments, fire damage liability to others, liquor liability, employee benefits liability, and herbicide and pesticide application liability, where the club is legally obligated to pay for an occurrence.

- **Business Auto Insurance** protects against loss if the club is held legally liable for bodily injury, death, or property damage to others caused by accident involving club-owned, nonowned, or hired vehicles. Be sure that the policy covers occurrences by a staff member or officer driving his own car on club business.

- **Property Insurance** protects against direct or consequential loss resulting from "all risks," except earthquake, flood, or nuclear hazard. This coverage should include employee dishonesty and electronic data losses. The coverage should also provide for lost revenue due to fire or other damage so as to be able to keep core employees on payroll during the shutdown. Most policies have a requirement that the insurance coverage be at least eighty percent of the replacement cost of the structures covered. It is important to have the buildings appraised from time to time so the insurance limits are sufficient. With a good appraisal, the insurance company should waive the eighty percent requirement.

- **Directors and Officers Liability Insurance** protects the club, its officers, and directors from claims arising from board action.

- **Storage Tank Third-Party Liability, Corrective Action, and Clean-up Insurance** protects against claims arising from underground tanks.

- **Umbrella Coverage Insurance** increases the policy limits on all of the club's liability insurance.

The board should inquire as to whether the club's insurance protects the club and its officers and directors from claims of discrimination in all forms. The board should also determine the need for flood insurance.

Your bylaws should contain language indemnifying the club's directors from all legal liability (see Article X, Section 3 of the Model Bylaws found in the Appendix). Nonetheless, and no matter how strong that language, I would advise against anyone serving on a board that does not protect its board members with D&O coverage.

With all forms of insurance, it is important to notify the insurance carrier as soon as someone makes a claim, or even when a claim is merely on the horizon. Failure to give proper notice can result in a denial of coverage. A typical policy, for example, specifies: "Upon knowledge of discovery by an officer of loss or an occurrence *which may become* a loss [the emphasis is my own], written notice shall be given to the insurance company at the earliest practical moment, and in no event later than 60 days after such discovery."

Occasionally a question arises as to whether a claim is covered under the club's insurance policy. In such a case, the insurance carrier may defend the claim under a "reservations of rights" notice given to the insured. This means the company, by defending, is not waiving any of its rights to later say there is no insurance coverage. If such a notice is received, the club should seek counsel from the club's lawyer on how to proceed. ▲

Guarding the Door

5

Well-written bylaws must define the criteria for membership and provide a mechanism for the admission of candidates, while at the same time avoiding language that might make the club vulnerable in a court of law.

The Bylaws, By Law

The term "bylaw" comes from Norse origins, tracing its roots to the ancient "byr," for "village." Middle English dropped the "r" to coin "bylawe," or "bilawe," but the idea remained the same. Bylaws are codified customs—the standard operating procedures of a group.

In modern usage, the "by" in bylaws also means secondary, in that they are always subject to higher law. For private clubs, this means that the policies and procedures specified in the bylaws cannot conflict with the club's articles of incorporation, with civil or criminal laws of the municipality and state within which the club functions, or with federal laws (civil and criminal) of the United States.

Under current federal law, all clubs enjoying the tax benefits of "nonprofit" status under §501(c)(7) of the Internal Revenue Code—roughly seventy percent of all private clubs—are prohibited from discriminating on the basis of race, religion, or national origin (but not gender).

By the Book

No board member can govern effectively without an understanding of the terms of governance as outlined in the club bylaws.

The bylaws set the form of governance for the club. They describe the rights of membership, the discipline of members, and how the board is elected and its powers and limitations. The bylaws also describe when the consent of the membership must be obtained and the procedure for amendment. The good board member should study the bylaws and be familiar with every detail.

Every club has its own distinctive set of bylaws, and the older the club the more distinctive the bylaws will be due to amendments made over the years. Hence, there is no one model applicable to all clubs. The main distinction among clubs is: Does the member have ownership rights that allow some refund when the membership is terminated or does the member walk away with nothing upon termination of the membership?

In the Appendix, see a set of Model Bylaws giving members a return on part of their membership investment. Many of the provisions are applicable to most clubs. These bylaws will be referred to from time to time throughout the text and may serve as a guide as you examine your own bylaws. ▲

State antidiscrimination laws serve to fill in any perceived loopholes in federal statutes. Maryland law adds gender discrimination to the forbidden mix, denying state tax benefits to any club barring members of either sex. The state of New York also bars gender discrimination for any organization with more than four hundred members, regardless of tax status. Under Utah law, a club can discriminate all it wants, but the state will deny it a license to serve liquor on club premises.

In Massachusetts and Pennsylvania, any private club that qualifies as a "public accommodation" is required not to discriminate as to gender. Having outside events can qualify the club as a public accommodation. One club in Massachusetts found itself facing a judgment against it (including interest and attorney's fees) of approximately four million dollars because of discrimination against women. The decision is on appeal, but the club was required to rewrite its bylaws to ensure equal rights for men and women.

Four decades' worth of court actions have challenged clubs' traditional rights of exclusion. Such challenges have produced U.S. Supreme Court rulings that limit the constitutional guarantees of free speech and assembly under which many private clubs blatantly practiced discrimination over many generations.

The broadening of antidiscrimination law has also affected the operations of clubs that have never discriminated against membership-candidates from any of the protected categories. All clubs discriminate in one way or another, if only in that they restrict membership to those able to pay entrance fees and annual dues.

But the area between what is "acceptable" discrimination and what is not has become a minefield. If the town drunk (or its street-fighting bully) hits the Lotto and has the money to join up, does your club have to let him in? What if he's Asian, or Muslim, or black? What if he's a she?

The one instrument that boards have for negotiating this dangerous terrain is the club bylaws. Well-written bylaws must define the criteria for membership and provide a mechanism for the admission of candidates, while at the same time avoiding language that might make the club vulnerable in a court of law.

In the Model Bylaws presented in the Appendix, notice that Article XI, Section 4 provides considerable detail on the application-and-acceptance parts of the membership process. On the question of who gets in and who doesn't, however, the bylaws say that the board will "only approve applicants of good moral character and reputation who are deemed compatible with present members."

Nowhere do they say that the board must approve *all* upright applicants. Nor is there any explanation of who gets to determine an applicant's "compatibility." If three or more board members vote against the applicant, he's history. It's as simple as that (provided that the denial of membership is not made on the basis of prohibited discrimination).

Club bylaws do at least need to be specific when it comes to defining the basic parameters of membership. However, a club that has substantial outside events open to nonmembers can find itself being governed by the laws relating to "place of public accommodation." Here the rules against discrimination are much broader in scope and the club's freedom of choice in membership can be severely limited.

Nuts and Bolts

If bylaws generally leave open the question of how individuals are approved for membership, well-drawn bylaws should be specific about the *mechanics* of membership. Otherwise, in the absence of defined policy regarding such matters as the transference of membership in the event of death or divorce, much of the board members' time may be taken up in resolving questions on a case-by-case basis.

If you're working within bylaws that aren't as clear-cut as the sample shown in the Appendix, make sure you at least understand the board's policy for dealing with the issues raised, which should be in writing and fairly applied.

Dues, Fees, and Assessments

However lavish its clubhouse or magnificent its golf course, a club's membership is still its most valuable asset. The membership is the club's revenue base, after all—the principal source of the money it takes to care for the clubhouse, maintain the golf course, keep the kitchen open and the bar pouring, and pay the staff.

Dues: The setting of member dues is the most visible function of the club board and potentially the most controversial. It is here that the conflict between the fiscal conservative and the more liberal members of the board will show itself. Some members want to cut expenses and even services while others want to expand services. Many times the break will come between the older members, who are usually most able to afford dues increases but tend to resist them most vehemently, and the younger members, some of whom have their dues paid for by their company or business.

Typically, the bylaws will specify a cap on the club's ability to raise dues more than a certain percent in any given year, but in a few clubs the board will have full latitude to set whatever dues it feels appropriate. At the very least, though, the bylaws should provide for the equitable determination of dues according to membership category.

Unless otherwise specified by the bylaws, it is understood that revenues from the membership's annual dues go into the club's general fund to cover day-to-day operating costs, which will include expenses for repair and replacement of the facilities and may include some capital improvements.

Fees: But what about initiation fees, which usually represent a substantial secondary source of club income? (In one respect, at least, initiation fees are even a superior source of income: membership equity contributions are often refundable in whole or in part; initiation fees are not.)

Often, club bylaws will direct the handling of initiation fees, specifying that a percentage (up to one hundred percent) of those funds be set aside for one or another specific purpose. Most major accounting firms that serve the club industry think that initiation fees should go into a capital improvement fund rather than be used as operating income.

Assessments: Assessments, the third category of revenue sources overseen by the board, are the board's special recourse for situations of acute need, including major capital improvements. Generally, the power to levy an assessment on the membership is restricted by express stipulations in the bylaws.

Notice in the Model Bylaws shown in the Appendix that the Takhomasak board can levy an assessment of no more than ten percent of a member's annual dues. If the board proposes a larger assessment, it must seek the approval of a majority of the membership voting on the issue. It should also discuss the matter with the club's attorney, as specified in "When to Call Your Lawyer" in the previous chapter.

Notice too that Article VII, Section 5 stipulates "a majority of the members voting on such an assessment." If an assessment is for adding tennis courts, say, then usually the assessment will be levied only on those whose memberships include use of the tennis facilities. In the case of the Takhomasak Club, that would include all Full Equity and Tennis Equity members.

But the Takhomasak bylaws make a common error. As written, *all* members get to vote on *all* assessments. In other words, members can vote to spend money they won't personally be charged.

Collections

While the board sets dues, fees, and assessments, collection of club accounts is usually the function of the club staff. When collection problems arise, however, the board functions as a council of last resort.

It is the board that must decide what action to take when a member's account has become seriously past due. The best bylaws should spell out precisely what length of time constitutes "serious" delinquency and will outline a procedure for dealing with such an account.

If your bylaws are not so specific, the board should adopt a standard operating procedure for governing the matter of delinquency. You don't want to be making decisions on a case-by-case basis. That's a sure recipe for trouble.

Terminating a membership and sending a past-due account out for collection is the ultimate option, of course, but usually the bylaws will recommend a set of internal actions first. These actions do not have to be sophisticated to be effective. Many clubs find that conspicuously posting the names of delinquent members is the best tactic for inducing payment in full. Often, a letter telling the member that his name will be posted if the account is not brought up to date will suffice.

However, posting the names of delinquent members presents a few hazards if it's not done right. Put yourself in the shoes of Joe Tardy, who's dining with his favorite client at the club when he finds his name prominently listed as delinquent on his club bill. (I've worn those shoes, in fact; this actually happened to me some years ago.)

Joe sues his club for defamation (which I did not), claiming

> Think of yourself as running a business, which you are. No business can survive if its management does not make every effort to safeguard revenues.

injury to his reputation. In some instances, Joe might have a case—unless the club's bylaws expressly permit the public posting of delinquent accounts, in which case Joe has implicitly consented by joining.

What if a posted delinquency is wrong? Mistakes happen, although this is not one that your accounting department should be allowed to repeat. Even in such unfortunate instances, the club has a legal defense if the action was reasonably based and in good faith, even if it was wrong.

To fully protect your club against liability from defamation, make sure that the bylaws spell out when and in what manner delinquencies will be posted. Make sure that your membership is aware of the policy, perhaps by incorporating it into your membership application forms. Enforce the policy strictly, with no exceptions.

Go the extra distance to make sure that postings are accurate. Post the notice where only members will see it. It's never a good idea to post delinquencies in a club newsletter, which often circulates to individuals outside the club.

When accounts go unpaid for a predetermined period of time, the bylaws should give the club the right to terminate the membership and sell the membership equity. Further, the bylaws should specifically authorize the club to deduct any monies due the club from any monies due the member from the sale of his equity.

The board should not be squeamish about applying all possible pressure to delinquent members. Think of yourself as running a business, which you are. No business can survive if its management does not make every effort to safeguard revenues. ▲

▲   Part Two   ▲

Getting to Work

Choosing a Leader

The presidency is a big job to give someone you hardly know, but in most cases that's the challenge new board members face at their very first board meeting.

Chairman Who?

Ironically, a new member's first official task is likely the very one that requires the most board experience to do well: elect a president.

Nothing is more important to the effective functioning of a board than the selection of someone to lead it. Specific powers and duties may vary according to club bylaws, but at the very least the president or chairman is always the club's chief executive officer, with all the powers and responsibilities that title entails. (These powers and responsibilities are distinct from those of the club's chief operating officer—its general manager—but more on that delicate balance of power in Chapter 11.)

The president or chairman presides over all club meetings, serves as an *ex officio* member on all club committees, appoints committee chairmen, and signs all official club documents.

He is responsible for communicating to the general membership all board actions—from raising dues, to broadening the membership base, to whether or not to keep the club bar open on Christmas Eve. The president acts as the official spokesperson for the club, its principal representative to the public. Internally, he serves as the principal liaison between the membership and club management.

It is the president's job to focus, unite, and mobilize the board, define its agenda, and thus set the club's course for the period of his term—usually a year, often with a two-term limit.

The presidency is a big job to give someone you hardly know, but in most cases that's the challenge a new board member faces at his very first meeting. Even though board members may know each other socially or from the golf course, they are not likely to be familiar with one another's administrative skills.

Some clubs try to have a chairman in place before the new board meets, perhaps by having the outgoing board choose the next year's president, or by throwing open the election to the general membership, so that a general vote designates not only the new board but its leader. I can't recommend either of these tactics.

Some clubs maintain a "ladder of leadership" system by which one year's vice president automatically becomes president the following year. If this is your club's choice, make sure the bylaws reflect it. Again, though, I prefer that each board be allowed to elect its own slate of officers. If the vice president has done his job well, he'll probably be elected president, anyway—but let the board decide.

Absent any persuasive alternative, then, one of the first things you'll do as a board member is elect your chairman or president. The process likely will be well under way by the time the new board convenes. There will almost always be a candidate from among the holdovers on the board, and usually veteran board members are an excellent choice. Certainly there is something to be said for electing a president who knows his or her way around club governance.

But be careful. Sometimes board members are elected again and again to maintain a status quo that, however popular with the membership, is no longer appropriate to the club's circumstances.

Board experience is a valid criterion for selecting a board president but not the only one.

Board experience is a valid criterion for selecting a board president but not the only one.

Occasionally, a new board member will be confronted with a choice between two opposing candidates from ranks of holdover governors. Board holdovers may be divided into sharply partisan camps, and the politicking of new members for their support may be intense. Do not allow yourself to be drawn into a rivalry that threatens to produce a disgruntled minority. Better to put your support toward a compromise candidate who may not ignite member passions but doesn't provoke resentments either.

As soon as you are notified of the time and place of your first board meeting, ask the outgoing chairman whether candidates for office have declared themselves. If so, request a resumé for each of the contenders. You might also ask that the chairman notify all board members that anyone standing for election should distribute a resumé prior to the meeting.

If his board term is to continue, the outgoing chairman will preside at the meeting up to the election of his successor, which is usually the first item of business to be considered. (If the outgoing chairman is not a board holdover, then the vice president, if a holdover, may preside—unless he is a candidate for the office.)

The chairman should open the floor to nominations, allow brief presentations by each candidate, and then call for a vote. If there are two or more nominees for any post, the balloting should be secret. Do not be deterred if that's not the way your club has traditionally elected its officers. At an appropriate point in the discussion, any member can propose that the vote be by written ballot and confidential. Do so—it will avoid complications later on. When there is only one candidate for any post, a voice vote will suffice.

Making Your Choice

The process of choosing club officers is too important to rush, so that item of business should dominate your first board meeting. When there is a contest for the job, candidates for the presidency

> No matter how great the temptation, don't short-change your club by electing a president who you know will end up rushed and preoccupied.

should make brief statements to the board. A list of three questions might be prepared in advance, with each candidate given the opportunity to respond to them within a preset time limit. Board members then have a chance to ask questions of each candidate, again within time constraints.

Before voting begins, the chairman may choose to recess the meeting for twenty minutes or so, so members can discuss the candidates informally. This time-out also gives members a quiet moment or two for private deliberation and an opportunity for the inevitable politicking.

- When considering a candidate for board president, first be sure that the individual you choose is able to devote the time necessary to do the job well.

  Preparing for and presiding over all board meetings, reviewing committee activities (and often attending committee meetings), dealing with individual member concerns, and maintaining open channels of communication with club management (a weekly lunch isn't a bad idea)—it can take a minimum of twenty to thirty hours a month to be an effective club president. And that's not even counting the time spent in board meetings—nor the time spent on the telephone listening to member complaints.

  Sadly, the most qualified candidates are often individuals who simply do not have three or four days a month to spare. No matter how great the temptation, however, don't short-change your club by electing a president who you know will end up rushed and preoccupied.

- Choose somebody smart. The president must be the sort of person who can grasp two sides of an issue, bringing even the most starkly conflicting viewpoints into a conciliatory focus, and that takes intelligence. Your club will be best served by a far-thinking, politically savvy president with a well-considered vision of the club's values, aspirations, and goals.

- Avoid any candidate with an ax to grind. Presidents are permitted to have positions on all the various matters under board consideration, but avid partisanship on the part of the chairman is inappropriate. It is not the president's job to impose his or her will on the board but to seek the will of the board and then see to it that it is met. "First among equals" is an apt description of the president's appropriate role.

That's not to suggest that the president should play a passive role in board proceedings. The ideal president is a leader, not a follower. He's got his own ideas and a vision for the club, and he's not reluctant to express himself. When the consensus of the board chooses a path other than what he has supported, however, a good president always falls into line with the will of his peers.

- Choose a president who is a good communicator—somebody who can articulate problems and express solutions in language that is clear to the board and the general membership. A gift for language can be an important asset for a club president, both in his or her role as administrator and as the club's chief mobilizer. A skilled communicator not only knows how to talk but is also a good listener. Avoid the presidential candidate who is too enamored of his own voice to hear the whispers at the other end of the table.
- Elect a president with a sense of humor. I do not mean the man who opens every meeting with a joke and spews one-liners throughout the proceedings (entertaining as that may be), but someone who can diffuse a tense situation with a humorous word or attitude. Take care to avoid the candidate who takes the club—and himself—too seriously; he or she may not be able to withstand the criticism that is an inevitable part of the job.

Corrective Action

You will never know how critical it is for an organization to have a good president until you have been part of a group with a bad one.

You'll recognize the symptoms. Meetings will run long and accomplish little. Action will be deferred repeatedly. Attendance

> You will never know how critical it is for an organization to have a good president until you have been part of a group with a bad one.

will become spotty, with members straggling in and out at will. Tempers and ill feelings will flare up from time to time.

Most club bylaws include some procedure for removal of an elected officer (see Article VI of the Model Bylaws in the Appendix), but these are rarely utilized. Nor should they be, because such actions usually cause the membership to lose confidence in the board as a whole. Except in extraordinary circumstances—felonious conduct, say, or some direct violation of the club charter and bylaws, or a degree of contentiousness bordering on mental instability—the club board has little recourse in the event of a bad president. You're stuck.

But there are steps that board members can take to somewhat mitigate the effects of bad leadership. For example, meetings can be pushed to action by an end-run around a stalled president using parliamentary rules. Members can agree among themselves to push for adoption of certain measures or to oppose others, thereby creating a unified force for action. It is here that a solid knowledge of parliamentary rules can be an enormous help.

Some offenses are more serious and may require that the board adopt a more confrontational approach. A president who repeatedly intrudes himself into what should be the decisions of the general manager, for example, can create havoc among paid staff as well as the board. If the president does not understand his appropriate role and behaves like a martinet—running roughshod over the general manager, attempting to direct day-to-day operations, creating his own policies, ignoring the board—board members may wish to delegate one of their own for a private discussion with the president about his conduct. If this does not work, then there is no alternative but to bring the matter up for consideration before the full board.

Sometimes a simple board resolution can do the trick. A member might propose that the board formally state its position, i.e., "The board hereby resolves that its members shall not involve themselves in those matters specifically assigned to the general manager." Or, "The board hereby resolves that none of its members may issue statements of a new club policy without the expressed consent of the board as a whole."

Whatever the disagreements within the board may be, and however intense they may become, the loyal member will keep them private, as with all board deliberations. There is no need for the general membership to know the housekeeping details of board service. The board should at all times maintain a united front before the membership.

> The board should at all times maintain a united front before the membership.

Club Committees

Club committees are like zebras. They come in many stripes and you can see in some of them traces of their cousin, the mule. There are also times when it's a good idea to keep them penned in.

In the past, many of the older clubs were ruled by committees. The club manager reported to the House Committee, the golf professionals reported to the Golf Committee, and the golf course superintendent reported to the Greens Committee. Today, most clubs have adopted the policy that the committees are advisory to the board and do not make or carry out policy decisions. That function is left to the elected board.

"Standing committees" are created by direction of the club bylaws and operate under a job description *specifically* defining their rights and responsibilities. "Ad hoc" committees (from the Latin "for this") are created by the board to perform a *specific* task, at the conclusion of which they are disbanded.

Note my emphasis here on being specific. If the bylaws do not define the job of each standing committee, the board should either amend the bylaws or attach a clarifying statement to each committee's charter. Unrestrained committees tend to stray into adjacent territory—Property into Greens, and so forth. Committee-overlap not only wastes time, it can strain tempers.

Committees serve a valuable function for any club. They provide expertise, dedication, and sound advice to the board, and they provide a fertile field for the nourishment of future club leaders. But a runaway committee can be a critical problem for club governance.

Mindful of the tendency of committees to run free of their boundaries occasionally, some clubs select their committee chairmen out of the membership of the board. While this certainly facilitates communication between a club board and its committees, it also limits a meaningful avenue of participation by the general membership in club governance and stifles the natural emergence of future leaders.

Perhaps the best solution is for the board to designate a liaison from its own membership to each of the club's committees. The committees function independently—and thus must keep and disseminate their own minutes—but their activities can be monitored, and at times directed, by an individual who provides a direct pipeline to the board.

Article V of the Model Bylaws (shown in the Appendix) spells out the job descriptions of the major committees of a country club and emphasizes in Section 4 the limitations on the powers of the committee. ▲

Meetings and How to Survive Them

No sport played on course, court, or field can match the meeting for the passions it arouses in some of its most devoted participants. For them, meetings can be passionate contests to be played fiercely—even ferociously—to win.

How Often, How Long?

The best meetings are those that get right to the point, so I'll do that too. The best way for the board to utilize the limited time of its members most effectively is regimentation, regimentation, regimentation.

Regular board meetings should take place at the same time each month and should follow a prescribed agenda. The regularity of the schedule is important. It's easy to remember when meetings are, in the first place, and it eliminates the time-consuming business of trying to tailor individual meetings to busy schedules.

From my own experience, I have come to prefer meetings no longer than two to three hours. Three hours may not be long enough to handle all business of a particularly heavy schedule, but it is about as long as you can expect human beings to stay at attention for a single stretch. When necessary, be open to separating the resolution of old business and the consideration of new business into two sessions. And, if particularly substantial matters are to be addressed—the hiring of a general manager, for example—consider bringing the board

> Meetings must be set for a time when *all* members can attend, ideally when they are reasonably alert and not too rushed.

together in special session in addition to the regular monthly meeting.

The best time for a board meeting varies with the makeup of the board. For a club composed mostly of retirees, a morning meeting might be most suitable. For clubs whose board members are active in business or the professions, late afternoon meetings—starting at four o'clock or so—might ensure the best attendance. Remember that meetings must be set for a time when *all* members can attend, ideally when they are reasonably alert and not too rushed.

Here are some other guidelines I have found useful—a kind of Boardroom Twelve Commandments, if you will:

1. **Never serve cocktails before or during a meeting**. "Alcohol," noted George Bernard Shaw's Major Barbara, "enables Parliament to do things at eleven at night that no sane person would do at eleven in the morning." Whatever the time of your meeting, alcohol does not help. It may loosen up the membership, but those benefits will be offset by the inevitable deterioration of discipline.

2. **Start precisely on time**. Be in your place and ready to begin at the specified time. Nothing is more infuriating for a member who has arrived promptly than having to cool his heels while the stragglers take their places. Don't bring latecomers up to date on what they've missed; it only encourages them.

3. **Allow no "excused" absences**. The board is not in a position to judge a "good" excuse from a "bad." The member is either present or he's not. And if he's not, do not allow him to transfer his voting proxy to any other member of the board. Insist on prenotification of any unavoidable absences. If a member cannot attend the regular meeting for any reason whatever, he should extend the board the courtesy of letting them know ahead of time.

4. **Work from a written agenda**. A good, written agenda and information supporting the agenda is the road map to a

successful meeting. The agenda package should contain a list of the items to be taken up, minutes of the previous meeting, copies of all committee reports, and appropriate backup data for items to be discussed. If there's an important resolution to be discussed, make sure that its formal wording is included so that board members have adequate time to consider both the language and the intent.

5. **Distribute the agenda in advance**. For regular meetings, see that the written agenda gets into board members' hands five days before the meeting. At some point, members will need to review the matters up for discussion, preferably not during the meeting itself.

6. **Don't overload the agenda**. Limit the agenda to policy matters that can be resolved during the course of the meeting. A long agenda can be evidence that the board is caught up in the details of management rather than focusing on policy matters. Set action items of most consequence for the early part of the meeting, before anyone's eyes start to glaze over.

7. **Stay on the subject**. Board deliberations need to stay focused. Stick to the subject at hand and do not deviate.

8. **Allow only one speaker at a time**. Nothing can be accomplished if everyone is talking at once. No speaker should proceed until recognized by the chairman. If the chairman fails to keep order, any board member may invoke parliamentary procedure to remind the group which member has the floor. Avoid sidebar conversations; that private chat between two members down at the end of the table means that neither one of them can give full attention to the issue at hand.

9. **Discourage surprises**. Any request for board action should be formulated in advance by the person or committee urging the action. Tell the board what specific action is required. To the extent possible, every major issue should be discussed and resolved at the committee level before it reaches the board. Complicated resolutions should be prepared in writing, in advance.

> When a meeting becomes combat—when members are shouting themselves red or stomping out of the room—it cannot function as the consensus-building device it is supposed to be.

10. **Set time limits**. Be sure to leave adequate time for discussion, but set time limits for general board discussion on any topic. The typical allotment is half an hour, but do not vote to take any action unless you feel that the issue has been adequately explored. You can always table further discussion to the next meeting, after all. It's also not a bad idea to set reasonable limits on the amount of time any one person may hold the floor. The length of the meeting itself should be limited by prearrangement. Include the time of adjournment in the agenda—and stick to it. It's amazing how much can be accomplished quickly as the time for adjournment approaches.

11. **Keep it civil**. No sport played on course, court, or field can match the meeting for the passions it arouses in some of its most devoted participants. For them, meetings can be passionate contests to be played fiercely—even ferociously—to win. But a meeting from which either winners or losers emerge is one in which the greater good of the membership has been endangered by a clash of egos. When a meeting becomes combat—when members are shouting themselves red or stomping out of the room—it cannot function as the consensus-building device it is supposed to be.

12. **Follow parliamentary rules of procedure**. Your bylaws should state which of the two standard sets of procedure it has adopted: the classic *Robert's Rules of Order* or the newer and somewhat more streamlined Sturgis' *Standard Code of Parliamentary Procedure*. There is an eighty-page pamphlet recently published by The American Bar Association entitled *The Modern Rules of Order*, which attempts to condense meeting canons into 15 rules.

Meeting Alternatives

A club board is formally alive only when holding a duly consti-

Judge Not

In his recent bestseller *Ship of Gold* (Atlantic Monthly Press, 1998), Gary Kinder portrays meetings as "the intellectual heart" of the process by which adventurer Tommy Thompson devised his plan to locate the treasure of the long-lost ship *Central America*.

What made those meetings so good, Thompson tells Kinder, was that everyone felt free to speak his mind. "No one worried that he would be judged by what he said. Ideas were not divided into good or bad, only those that worked and didn't work. And although an idea might not work for several reasons, one point of that idea might have merit. But you couldn't pluck the ripe part if the whole idea went unspoken. . . ." ▲

tuted session. But some states (and club bylaws) now authorize board action without a meeting if *all* board members sign on to a specific resolution. (A simple majority will not suffice.) Although this tactic can be useful at times, it deprives the board of the give-and-take of a board meeting and should be used only in emergency situations or when a quorum is not available, due to vacations, for example. The signed resolution or action should be reflected in the minutes of the next meeting of the board.

In today's world, board meetings may be held by conference call. If an important matter is to come before the board and one or two members are out of town, they can participate fully if they are brought into the meeting by a speakerphone. If it's a single member, a direct call using a speakerphone is all that is required; if more than one member is involved, a call to a conference-call operator can bring all parties onto the speakerphone.

The question of whether an absent member may legally express his consent (or dissent) by fax or e-mail varies from state to state, and the law on this subject is evolving. A fax with a written signature is probably sufficient for club purposes, but the board member should mail his consent with the original signature to confirm

General Robert and His Rules

Robert's Rules were devised by Henry M. Robert, a young Union officer during the Civil War who codified and simplified the rules of procedure of the U.S. House of Representatives. In 1876, Robert, by then a general, adapted the House rules to fit other civic organizations and published his manual (*Robert's Rules of Order*) for meeting conduct.

In 1950, Robert's Rules were rewritten and simplified by Alice Sturgis in an effort to eliminate deadwood that had accumulated over the years. Her manual, the *Standard Code of Parliamentary Procedure* (universally known as "Sturgis"), is now in its third edition, issued in 1988.

The two procedures differ in ways that are usually minor but can be significant. In Sturgis, for example, any member is permitted to move that a vote be reconsidered. In Robert's, only a member on the winning side of a resolution can move for reconsideration.

The intent of both Robert's and Sturgis is to maintain decorum, ascertain the will of the majority, protect the rights of the minority, and facilitate the orderly transaction of business. The essence of parliamentary rules is common sense and fair play. The rules contemplate reasonable, focused, and orderly discussion, followed by a decision. ▲

the fax. For legal reasons, e-mail consent should probably be followed by either a fax or letter with a signature affirming the action.

The chairman's role in a meeting is important. It is the responsibility of the chair to see that the meeting is conducted fairly, reasonably, and in a timely manner. Decisions of the chair are final on procedural matters, but any ruling of the chair can be reversed by a majority vote.

Parliamentary Rules in a Nutshell
(Applicable to both Robert's Rules and the Sturgis Code)
- If you want to *Introduce Business:*

Say, "I move that we . . ."
Can you interrupt a speaker to do so? No.
Is a second required? Yes.
Is the motion debatable? Yes.
Is it amendable? Yes.
What vote is needed? Majority.

- If you want to *Amend a Motion:*
Say, "I move to amend the motion by . . ."
Can you interrupt a speaker to do so? No.
Is a second required? Yes.
Is the motion debatable? Yes.
Is it amendable? Yes.
What vote is needed? Majority.

- If you want to *Withdraw a Motion:*
Say, "I move to withdraw my motion."
Can you interrupt a speaker to do so? Yes.
Is a second required? No.
Is the motion debatable? No.
Is it amendable? No.
What vote is needed? Majority.

- If you want a chance to *Study the Matter Further:*
Say, "I move we refer this matter to a committee."
Can you interrupt a speaker to do so? No.
Is a second required? Yes.
Is the motion debatable? Yes.
Is it amendable? Yes.
What vote is needed? Majority.

- If you want to *End Debate:*
Say, "I move we vote on the matter."
Can you interrupt a speaker to do so? No.
Is a second required? Yes.
Is the motion debatable? No.
Is it amendable? No.
What vote is needed? Two-thirds.

- If you want to *Delay Further Consideration:*
Say, "I move we table the matter."

Can you interrupt a speaker to do so? No.
Is a second required? Yes.
Is the motion debatable? No.
Is it amendable? No.
What vote is needed? Majority.

- If you want to *Take a Break:*
Say, "I move that we recess for fifteen minutes."
Can you interrupt a speaker to do so? No.
Is a second required? Yes.
Is the motion debatable? No.
Is it amendable? Yes.
What vote is needed? Majority.

- If you want to *Protest a Procedure or Statement:*
Say, "I rise to a point of order," or simply "Point of order."
Can you interrupt a speaker to do so? Yes.
Is a second required? No.
Is the motion debatable? No.
Is it amendable? No.
What vote is needed? None; action is at the discretion of the chair.

- If you want to *Take Up a Previously Tabled Matter:*
Say, "I move we take from the table . . ."
Can you interrupt a speaker to do so? No.
Is a second required? Yes.
Is the motion debatable? No.
Is it amendable? No.
What vote is needed? Majority.

- If you want to *Consider a Matter Out of its Scheduled Order:*
Say, "I move we suspend the rules and consider . . ."
Can you interrupt a speaker to do so? No.
Is a second required? Yes.
Is the motion debatable? No.
Is it amendable? No.
What vote is needed? Two-thirds.

- If you want to *Request Information:*
Say, "Point of information."
Can you interrupt a speaker to do so? Yes.

Is a second required? No.
Is the motion debatable? No.
Is it amendable? No.
What vote is needed? None.

- If you want to *Adjourn the Meeting:*
Say, "I move we adjourn."
Can you interrupt a speaker to do so? No.
Is a second required? Yes.
Is the motion debatable? No.
Is it amendable? No.
What vote is needed? Majority.

Some additional notes: If a motion is made but not seconded, the motion is automatically lost. Only two amendments to a motion are permitted before a vote must be taken on the last amendment. From there, action moves to the first amendment and then to the main motion.

All amendments must be germane to the main motion; otherwise the chair may rule the proposed amendment out of order. In an informal setting, a motion can be amended by agreement between the maker of the main motion and the one who seconded the main motion. This then becomes the main motion.

A motion to reconsider can be made by any board member under the Sturgis Code but only by a board member on "the prevailing side" under Robert's Rules. The motion is debatable but not amendable and must be made at the same meeting where the original motion was adopted. If done at a later meeting, the proper motion is a motion to rescind.

Sometimes a meeting can get so confused by motions, amendments, and other motions that neither the chair nor the board members know how to proceed. One way to get out of such gridlock is the "Gordian Knot" motion, which proposes to "suspend the rules" to permit the board to start afresh on the matter.

The Gordian Knot motion can usually be taken by consent. If an objection is made, the motion to suspend the rules cannot be amended and is not debatable. It requires a second and a two-thirds vote.

A concluding note on the use of parliamentary rules: A rigid enforcement of the rules can have the effect of turning the meeting inside out with emphasis on form rather than substance. A wise

Faces in the Boardroom

Even with a well-prepared agenda, you should have an understanding of the cast of characters generally present at a meeting. Otherwise, you will wonder why the meeting wandered and went nowhere. In the tale of Snow White, there are seven dwarfs. The club board has its modern equivalent. Here is my idea of the classic personalities found at most meetings:

The Submariner (Dopey)

He'll sit, say nothing, and vote against the proposal. No reasons given. What is he thinking? A few strategic questions from the chair may bring him to the surface.

The Know-It-All (Grumpy)

He attempts to overwhelm the meeting with his own ideas on every matter that comes before the board. No question is left unanswered. Many times he wanders outside the issues. The chair needs to put blinders on him and make him stay in focus. Also, he should be ignored when he tries to get the floor after each member has spoken. The chair needs to be firm with this guy so all members can speak.

The Loud Speaker (Happy)

This guy never met a decibel he didn't like and is delighted at the sound of his own voice. Volume overtakes logic. A gentle rap on the knuckles may bring him in tow.

The Filibusterer (Sneezy)

He dominates the floor in hopes of winning the point by exhaustion alone. He loves to criticize someone else's ideas and doesn't hesitate to bruise feelings. The chair really needs to put a handkerchief to this guy.

The Sleeper (Sleepy)

> He never says anything but sits back, eyes closed. He has a pensive look on his face but is actually half asleep. Most of the time he'll go along with the proposal. Don't wake him up. He's a valuable vote.

The Devil's Advocate (*not* Bashful)

> Everything is debatable with him. He brings up all of the negatives and at times can ferret out the truth. He's a good man to have aboard, but, please, only one devil at a time.

The Statesman (Doc)

> He's the one who does his homework, understands the issues, and is shrewd on handling his fellow members' feelings. That board member should be you.

Lastly (and one more than seven):

The Joker

> This clown sees every meeting as an opportunity to try out new stand-up material. Call on him when things get hot, but after three minutes, shut him down. ▲

chairman will know when to insist on following the parliamentary rules and when to go with the flow on an informal basis. When things are contentious, the rules can help sort things out. When the meeting is going smoothly and there is little dissent, the literal following of the parliamentary rules need not be insisted upon.

Long before Robert's Rules, Thomas Jefferson, while vice president of the U.S., wrote parliamentary rules for the Senate. Rule 17.9 required, "No one is to speak impertinently or beside the question, superfluously or tediously." ▲

Keeping Accurate Records

8

The most important function of the minutes is to record all motions or resolutions that have been adopted, preferably in the language used during the meeting itself. . . . Minutes are not a transcript of discussion but a record of action.

For the Record

Communication with the membership remains the most obvious function of today's club board minutes but it is important to remember that they are also the backbone of a club's history, its institutional memory.

And they are a legal record. In the event of litigation, courts give great weight to the official minutes, and auditors depend on them as proof of authorization for expenditures. Under the law, minutes are evidence, pure and simple.

The minutes of a club board meeting should begin with the following:

- The date, time, and place of the meeting, and the time at which it was adjourned.
- Explanation of whether the session recorded is a regular meeting or a special meeting. If a special meeting, a copy of the notice announcing it should be attached.

- The names of the members present, those absent, the presiding officer, and the individual recording the minutes. In the event that a board member arrives after action has been taken, or leaves early, this should be recorded as well—not for any punitive reasons but simply to acknowledge that Member X may not have been present for the entirety of discussion on a matter.

> Minutes of the previous meeting should be distributed far enough in advance so that board members have sufficient opportunity to review the record before voting to approve it.

- Acknowledgment that a quorum was present for the session. This is simply a formality, since under most club bylaws, if there's no quorum, there's no meeting—and hence no reason to record its actions, which carry no authority.
- Notice that the minutes of the board's previous session were read and approved as presented or amended.

Read Before You Sign

Most meetings will begin with a call for approval of the minutes of the previous meeting. Each member should read the minutes thoroughly before voting to approve. Often, in an effort to impose order on the verbal chaos of a meeting, the recording secretary will have to paraphrase a motion or resolution, and sometimes the original intent of the motion or resolution may be inadvertently misstated.

I remember all too well a circumstance involving a club board that believed it had finally settled a long-standing jurisdictional dispute between the Greens Committee and the Property Committee. Each believed itself to be in charge of the golf course equipment.

After much heated discussion, the board decided to give the Property Committee responsibility for all equipment relating to the golf course. In transcription, however, the secretary inadvertently omitted the action, resulting in a jurisdictional shouting match between two committee chairmen.

Ultimately, the board was able to extricate itself from the conse-

> Board minutes should be maintained for the life of the club.

quences of the error, but at the expense of several hours' worth of renewed discussion on a matter it thought already resolved.

Minutes of the previous meeting should be distributed far enough in advance so that board members have sufficient opportunity to review the record before voting to approve it. Ideally, the secretary will distribute the minutes of the last meeting with the written agenda for the next; one week ahead of time is optimal, though four days is typical.

In some clubs, the secretary will prepare a summary of major board actions shortly after a meeting and, after review by the president, post it for the general membership, clearly identified as a digest. (In one club, these are called "Fast Facts.") Remember that this summary carries no official weight. Minutes are not official until the board has agreed to accept them.

Acceptance of the minutes is usually accomplished "by consent," meaning that neither discussion nor a formal vote is required. In the event that amendment is required, this change can also be adopted by consent. Minor changes can be made by hand—be sure they are initialed by both the secretary and the chairman—and do not have to be acknowledged in the minutes of the meeting in which the change is made; a simple acknowledgment that "The minutes were accepted as amended" will suffice.

For more substantial changes, it is best to record them word for word on the record of the meeting in which they are made, i.e., "John Jones moved that the minutes of the previous meeting be amended as follows. . . ."

Approval of the minutes is not the time to readdress questions resolved at the last meeting. The only question at this time should be whether the minutes accurately portray the actions taken at the previous meeting.

After the minutes have been approved by the board and signed by both the secretary and the president, they should be placed in the club's permanent minute book. "Permanent" is the operative word here: board minutes should be maintained for the life of the club.

Some clubs now compile a computer archive of minutes; others maintain a master list of board policies gleaned from the minutes—indexed by subject matter and designating the dates of enactment—usually referred to as a "Policy Manual." Neither of these is a satisfactory substitute for bound volumes of signed, hard-copy minutes, but they can be very helpful in the day-to-day running of the club. The Policy Manual, for example, helps avoid rearguing matters previously decided and assists in maintaining consistency of policy as board members come and go.

The Official Version

The most important function of the minutes is to record all motions or resolutions that have been adopted, preferably in the language used during the meeting itself. The name of the board member originating the motion or resolution should be included. While all minutes should acknowledge that the motion or resolution was duly seconded, the name of the seconding member need not be specified unless club custom so indicates.

All amendments to the main motion or resolution—and the names of the persons making them—should be recorded separately, with the names of those proposing the amendment (and seconding it, if club custom so indicates). If all amendments are agreed to, only the final motion as amended need go into the minutes.

Recording the vote tally may not be necessary from a legal standpoint, but it makes it easier to move later for reconsideration of a motion approved or rejected by a tight vote (or makes it more difficult to cause reconsideration of a motion approved or rejected by a decisive vote). However, under Sturgis, any member may move to reconsider. The vote tally can also convey between-the-lines information to the membership—indecision on the part of the board or unambiguous solidarity, as the case may be.

Any board member who dissents from a board action has the right to have his dissent, and the reasons for it, noted in the record. A member may have the dissent inserted into the minutes by simply requesting it, and the request itself should be entered into the minutes, i.e., "Mr. Jones asked that the official record note his opposition to the motion as approved, with the following explanation. . . ."

In the event the board elects to take no formal action on a motion or resolution that has been seconded, the motion or resolution should be recorded in the minutes nonetheless, and its ultimate disposition—"tabled for later discussion," for example—should be specified.

The record should include the name of the board member proposing that no action be taken. If the decision is made unanimously, it is appropriate that it be designated as "the sense of the board," as in: "It was the sense of the board that the consideration of the motion be delayed, pending a report relevant to the matter by the Greens Committee."

Motions made but not seconded should not be acknowledged in the minutes, as it takes a formal second for any motion to be considered before the board.

Committee reports submitted during the course of a meeting should be acknowledged in the minutes, either as "accepted" (in which case the substance of the committee report should be written into the minutes, or the actual report attached) or "received" (which suggests a delay in final approval, pending some clarification or change in language). In the event that formal approval of the committee report is put off, the name of the individual proposing the delay should be specified in the minutes.

The "acceptance" of a committee report does not bind the board to its recommendations, by the way, but it's better to note a report as "received" rather than "accepted" in the event of any dispute over approval.

Too Much Detail

"Minutes are the indispensable record of the deliberations and decisions of a board," writes Cyril O. Houle in his book *Governing Boards* (Jossey-Bass, Inc., 1989).

"They provide the opportunity for [the membership] to learn about or be reminded of the board's actions.

"If minutes are not kept, or if they are sketchy and incomplete, confusion and conflict will almost inevitably result. Much time will be lost by disagreements among board members, the executives, and the staff about the exact nature of decisions taken, and by a repetition of earlier discussions, this time with the addition of acrimony."

> Minutes are not a transcript of discussion but a record of action.

Mr. Houle's excellent book does not mention it directly, but acrimony can result as well if minutes are *too* complete. Does the membership need to know the name of the board member proposing a special assessment for tennis-court lights when the motion died for lack of a second? Is it necessary to report what Member X and Member Y had to say about the alleged transgressions that resulted in the reprimand of Member Z? Should the minutes include offhand complaints made about the quality of service in the dining room?

No, no, and no. Both Robert's and Sturgis agree that minutes are not a transcript of discussion but a record of action. The role of the secretary is to "record what is done . . . not what is said," says Robert's. "In general," says Sturgis, "minutes are a record of all actions and proceedings but not a record of discussions."

By causing members to fear that their every word will be recorded, overly detailed minutes can freeze the free flow of board discussion. If it's in the minutes, keep in mind: any member has ready access to it.

In most states, the law is clear that any club member has the absolute right to see the approved club minutes—along with the articles of incorporation, the bylaws, and official membership rolls—at any time, without having to specify a reason for the request.

Executive Session

In sensitive matters such as member discipline, personnel issues, litigation, and censure of a board member, the board may wish to conduct its deliberations entirely off the record. The standard device available for this purpose is the "executive session"—a useful tool for discussion of subjects that are (or are perceived to be) confidential, sticky, embarrassing, or contentious.

A meeting or any part thereof can be moved into executive session by a two-thirds vote of the members. Essentially, the members vote to "suspend the rules" by switching from recorded business to

> Executive sessions should not become simply an opportunity for free-for-all grousing. Like meetings themselves, executive sessions should be action-oriented.

off-the-record consideration of a specific issue. (Typically, the general manager and any other employees or guests will be excluded from executive session, unless there is some compelling reason to ask that they remain.)

The motion to suspend, the name of the person proposing it, the presence of a second, and the vote of the directors should be acknowledged in the minutes. (If the vote is unanimous, it can be designated as "by consent.")

Some clubs keep notes on what transpires in executive session, but they are rarely reflected in the official minutes. These notes may be distributed to those members attending the session, or even to the full board, in which case the official minutes should contain some acknowledgment on the order of, "The notes of the board in executive session, held on January 17, 2004, were approved."

(Many states have adopted "Sunshine Laws," which prohibit public boards and some homeowner associations from having executive sessions except in limited situations, such as those involving litigation. As a general rule, such laws do not affect private clubs.)

Some club boards routinely earmark the final portion of their regular meetings for "executive session" to give members an opportunity to discuss anything they may want to get off their chests. This is, I think, a mistake on two counts.

Any subject worthy of executive session is too important to be given the closing spot on the agenda, when members may be too tired or restless to bring things to a close. And, executive sessions should not become simply an opportunity for free-for-all grousing. Like meetings themselves, executive sessions should be action-oriented.

If an executive session is scheduled on the agenda, it should be understood in advance that discussion will center on a particular concern. Board members should have the opportunity to prepare themselves for any subject to be considered in executive session.

The official minutes, though, can remain vague: "Mr. Jones proposed a matter for discussion in executive session at the next meeting. The motion was seconded and approved by a two-thirds vote of the board, and the executive session was duly scheduled for the April board meeting."

> If the board grants the request to tape, it should record the meeting on its own equipment as well.

To Tape or Not to Tape

The advent of electronic recording equipment has both streamlined and complicated the business of minutes. Today, many clubs tape record their board meetings; some even videotape them.

To allow the secretary to participate more fully in the meeting, minutes may be taken from the tape rather than during the meeting itself. In other cases, the tape is reserved as a backup for handwritten notes taken at the meeting by the club secretary or other designated person.

I believe that meetings should never be taped for any reason. (Several recent U.S. presidents would probably concur.) Remember that minutes are intended to be a record of action taken; any tape, inevitably, will include all the starts and stops of serious discussion plus all the offhand remarks and casual jokes that pepper the typical board session.

The presence of a tape recorder can stifle the free flow of any meeting. Anything that exists on tape becomes, by extension, part of the record, and therefore can be subpoenaed in the event of court litigation. Just as any member may request a copy of the board's minutes, he or she can request a hearing of the taped proceedings, and many courts would support such a request. One unintended consequence of tape recording is to increase the length of the minutes.

Unless there is an extraordinary reason to do so, no board member should be allowed to tape record a meeting with his own equipment. Such a request usually signals trouble of some kind. If the board grants the request to tape, it should record the meeting on its own equipment as well. Any board member discovered to have secretly taped a meeting should be dealt with severely.

What to Keep and for How Long

Here are my recommendations, based on established legal and accounting practices, with a dash of personal experience:

Keep permanently:

Annual report to members

Audit reports

Bylaws, including repealed and amended

Cashbooks

Charter

Charts of accounts

Canceled checks for important payments, i.e. taxes, purchase of property, long-term contracts, etc. (checks should be filed with the papers pertaining to the underlying transaction)

Club rules and policies

Major contracts and leases

Correspondence (legal and important matters)

Deeds, mortgages, and bills of sale

Depreciation schedules

Employee handbook and all amendments thereto

Financial statements (year-end; others optional)

General ledgers

Journals

Minutes of board and membership meetings

Property appraisals

Property acquisition records (including costs, depreciation schedules, blueprints, and plans)

Retirement and pension records

Tax returns and worksheets, revenue agents' reports, and other documents relating to determination of income tax liability

Letters of professional opinion from attorneys and accountants

Long-range plans

Keep for seven years:

Accounts payable ledgers

Accounts receivable ledgers and schedules

Canceled checks

Committee minutes and reports
Insurance policies (expired)
Payroll records and summaries
Personnel files on terminated employees
Purchase orders
Voucher register and schedules
Vouchers for payments to vendors, employees, etc.
Withholding tax statements

Keep for three years:
Bank statements
Employment applications
Internal audit reports (longer retention may be desirable)
Internal reports
Routine correspondence

Keep for two years:
Bank reconciliations
Correspondence (general)
Deposit slips

Handling Requests for Information

As previously noted, any club member has the absolute right to request at any time a copy of the most recent board minutes, the club bylaws, articles of incorporation, and membership rolls. In addition, under statute, a member may have the right to see other books and records (such as financial statements) if a valid reason is given.

The courts have construed the question of "valid reason" quite broadly, upholding again and again the right of any shareholder (or member, in the case of a club) to be intelligently informed about corporate affairs.

As for documents not covered by the rule of absolute right, club policy may require the member to specify in writing what records are being requested and to have and designate a proper purpose for making the request.

The purpose must be directly related to the documents being requested, i.e. "Because I question whether the Takhomasak Country Club, Inc. is properly amortizing its fixtures and equipment, I hereby request a copy of the Club's amortization schedule for the past three years." The right of inspection by a member extends to the member's attorney.

If the request is granted, the club can set a reasonable time and place for compliance. The requesting member may be required to pay the cost of copying the documents requested. In the event the request to be denied, counsel for the club should be consulted before the denial is issued. That a member is openly hostile toward the board or the general manager is not reasonable grounds to deny his request for information.

It should be noted that tax-exempt clubs are required to provide copies of their exemption documents to the public. ▲

Money Matters

The club's audited and certified financial statement should be read with extra care. Like an MRI or an X-ray, it sometimes provides the first warning of trouble.

Checking the Books

Every board member should expect to receive a monthly report from the club's treasurer or controller on the club's income and expenses, broken down by category (i.e., "Golf Services," "Food and Beverage").

In some clubs, the board reviews the full financial statement on a monthly basis. But the sheer bulk of such documents (which can run to twenty pages or more) is likely to overwhelm some board members to the extent that they ignore all the information given. Although any board member has the right to ask for the more detailed monthly report, summary reports (such as that in the sample shown on page 84) are usually more meaningful.

The board should review the club's audited and certified financial statement on an annual basis. This should be read with extra care. Like an MRI or an X-ray, it sometimes provides the first warning of trouble.

Most club financial reports are based on the *Uniform System of Accounts*, published by the Club Managers Association of America. This uniform system, which is useful as a ready comparison with other clubs, sets up standardized account categories for every aspect of club operation.

The audited statement will present the Annual Statement of Financial Position, comparing it dollar for dollar—asset to asset, liability to liability—with that of the previous year.

The year's Statement of Activities will be included, showing (in summary form) the source of all club revenues and expenses, including depreciation, and the net amount after deducting expenses from revenue. The statement will deduct depreciation, which reflects the aging of the club's capital assets (buildings and equipment) to give a figure that shows excess of revenue over expense—or the reverse.

The annual financial statement should include a review of members' equity (club assets less debts and liabilities) and a statement of cash flow (a detailed report of club revenue, with an explanation of where the revenue went). And it will likely contain a section entitled "Notes to the Financial Statements," which is largely an explanation of accounting policies and procedures and a mention of anything the accountants may have found unusual.

A letter from the accountants will state whether they conducted a full audit of the club's financial affairs or merely a review. The full audit investigates beyond the accounting records to verify inventory, cash on hand, and capital equipment, for example, and the auditors may spot-check the club's receivables and payables. The auditing firm puts its own reputation on the line by certifying the results in a full audit. In a review, the auditing firm relies more on the club's accounting records as presented.

Although more expensive, a full audit is the more reliable option and therefore preferable. An annual audit by an outside CPA firm is the best possible insurance that the board is carrying out its primary duty of protecting club assets.

What to Look For

Most board members are reasonably sophisticated in reading

financial statements and will know to be on the lookout for any anomalies or variations from the norm. What follows is a guide to the sort of questions you might ask as you study the financial documents.

- Is the CPA firm's "Letter to Management" included for board review? This is the place where auditors would mention weaknesses in internal control and accounting procedures discovered in the course of their investigation, and it is precisely these that the board should be aware of.

- Is the club "on budget"? Budgets are not hard-and-fast rules, but any substantial deviation from the budget—more than ten percent in any month—should be scrutinized closely and explanations demanded. (Many times, budget discrepancies are simply a matter of timing—a load of fertilizer budgeted for May arrives and is billed in April.)

- What are expense ratios on food and beverage costs (cost of food or beverage ingredients vs. price of food or beverage)? Food costs should not exceed 46 percent of sales; 45 percent is typical. If the club is spending more, there may be problems with pilferage, poor inventory control, or lax management that the board should address. Keep in mind that unless there is substantial outside income, the average private club loses money on its food and beverage operations. (Clubs in the Southeast typically run at a loss of 33 percent, whereas clubs in the North and Central areas average a 16-percent loss.) Prices have to be kept low to maintain member satisfaction, the restaurant and bar have to remain open even if there are no customers, and tables turn over less frequently than in public restaurants. The resulting shortfall has to be made up out of club dues. It is the board's duty to minimize the loss and to ensure that food-and-beverage service is of the quality that club members have a right to expect.

- What is the annual turnover rate for goods held for resale? Low-margin, high-volume retailers may turn over their entire inventory as often as twelve times a year. Few, if any, clubs ever ring up such sales on the pro shop items and whatnot that they sell, but it is not unreasonable to expect retail inventory to turn over at least twice in any year. Turnover is easily calculated as annual sales divided by inventory. If your pro shop has $100,000 at retail in inventory and annual sales of $200,000, then it has turned over its inventory twice.

- Is the club carrying over unsold merchandise each year? A season-end sale with substantial price reductions will keep the merchandise fresh and prevent a buildup of old inventory.
- What method is used to determine sale price on retailed items? Board policy should set a standard markup on all goods the club sells at retail. I think it's best to express that markup as a percentage of the cost, rather than of the sale price, because, as your accountants may tell you, this makes your figures compatible with other financial data. Thus, if a sport shirt in the pro shop costs the club $20 and sells at retail for $24, the markup is 20%—cost times markup percentage ($20 x 20% = $4, the markup). The markup divided by the selling price produces the gross margin ($4 ÷ 24 = 16½ %). So, when figuring from cost, the $4 markup is 20%. When figuring from selling price, the gross margin is 16½ %. In order to keep their prices attractive to members, many clubs use a standard markup of 20%.
- Are accounts receivable current? How many are past due?
- Are bills being paid to get the maximum discount?
- Does the club do co-op buying?
- Are special records kept for unrelated business income? (All clubs with §501(c)(7) tax status are required to keep such records, as discussed later in this chapter.)
- Are general overhead items allocated to various departments in the club?
- How does golf course maintenance compare with other clubs in the area? (McGladrey & Pullen of Ft. Lauderdale, Florida, among other companies, collects and sells such data.)
- What is the percentage of "outside income" to the total income? (Again, a critical number, as it affects §501(c)(7) status. Keep reading for details.)
- Is the club paying withholding taxes on time and in the manner prescribed by law?

- What is the status of the capital account funds?
- Is excess cash invested? Where? At what rate? For what term? Are investments FDIC-insured?

> It is important that board members have a general understanding of the tax principles that apply to private clubs.

Taxes

Since member-owned private clubs have had a long-standing special status in the world of taxation, it is important that board members have a general understanding of the tax principles that apply to private clubs.

It has been estimated that seventy percent of private clubs are tax-exempt. This means that about thirty percent of all clubs are taxed under normal corporate tax rules, sometimes to the surprise of their members.

Member-owned clubs (as distinguished from developer-owned or privately owned clubs) can claim tax exemption under Section §501(c)(7) of the Internal Revenue Code. The claim of exemption under §501(c)(7) is not automatic and must be applied for using IRS Form 1024. Nor is the exemption granted automatically; typically, extensive documentation is required.

(States vary on the taxation of private clubs. Many states exempt assessments for capital improvements from sales tax. In such states, if the annual budget used in setting dues includes an amount for capital improvements, this amount should be treated separately on the members' monthly bills and should not be subject to sales tax.)

To meet the federal exemption requirements under §501(c)(7), the following criteria must be met:

- The organization must be duly incorporated as a club. In defining a "club," the government puts great emphasis on memberships of individual persons, with characteristics of fellowship, personal contacts, and commingling among the members. A corporation may not be a member but may hold the underlying equity certificate with the power to designate an individual who *is* the member. Developer-owned clubs do

Hiring a CPA

All CPAs are accountants but not all accountants are CPAs. Depending on the professional-regulation laws of your state, it may be possible for an individual to sell his accounting services without having actually earned state certification of his skills and knowledge. You may save some money going this route, but, as with choosing an attorney to represent your club's legal interests, it's best not to nickel-and-dime on matters of economic security.

In addition to passing the test to get his initial certification, a CPA is required to continue his education through courses dealing with changes in the tax law, among other subjects. With a CPA, you should be able to expect that his knowledge is current at all times.

Never hire a CPA from within the club, which would at the very least create the appearance of compromised independence. It's best to choose an accountant with no relationship at all to the club.

Make use of your CPA not only for his annual audits but also for his advice on tax and other financial matters throughout the year. If the club is considering a major capital expenditure program, for example, your accountant may be able to prepare a *pro forma* income and expense statement and balance sheet that would project into the future what the financial impact of such a program would be. You'll find it much easier to get the approval of your membership if you can demonstrate precisely what the capital program will mean to them. ▲

not qualify for §501(c)(7) status.

- It must be organized for pleasure, recreation, or other non-profit purposes.
- Substantially all of the activities of the club must be for such purposes. No more than fifteen percent of the gross income

of the club may be derived from the general public's use of the club facilities or services.

- No part of the earnings shall accrue to the benefit of the shareholders.
- The charter, bylaws, club rules, and any written club policy must not discriminate against a person on the basis of race, color, or religion. (Note that discrimination by reason of gender is not expressly prohibited, although the current trend in case law and state legislation tends to prohibit sex discrimination in many club cases.)

Some clubs that would otherwise qualify for tax exemption have elected to be taxed as regular for-profit corporations. Among these are clubs whose combined expenses and depreciation exceed revenues, thus giving them no taxable income. For other clubs, the tax benefits of §501(c)(7) are less important than that club members remain free to do what they want to do—such as generate unlimited outside income or restrict membership based on race or religion.

"Tax-exempt" is a relative term. Like any other employer, clubs must withhold income and other taxes from employees' wages and pay those amounts to the federal and state governments on a regular basis. And states vary widely on the taxation of private clubs. In some states—Florida, for example—club dues are subject to state sales tax, while capital assessments are exempt.

The bottom line of taxation of clubs electing §501(c)(7) treatment is that member-related income is not subject to tax *unless* the amount of unrelated outside income for use of club facilities exceeds fifteen percent. If it exceeds fifteen percent, then *all* of the club's net income is subject to tax. However, even if the club is under the fifteen-percent maximum, all of the outside income from use of club facilities is subject to the unrelated business income tax (UBIT).

For clubs granted §501(c)(7) status, income—dues, payments for club goods or services (such as food and beverages), equipment in the pro shop, or "door charges" for social or sports activities—is exempt if it originates from members, their dependents, and/or their guests. If the club is venturing away from the norm into non-traditional activities (such as outside catering or selling wine or liquor by the case) or is heavily into the banquet business or non-member events (such as golf outings), bells should be ringing in the mind of every board member.

Under what is known as The Rule of Eight—where a group of eight or fewer individuals (at least one of whom is a member) uses the facilities of the club and payment is received from the member or the member's employer—it is assumed for audit purposes that all of the non-members are guests of the member and not part of the general public. Thus, this income would not be considered taxable as unrelated business income. Likewise, where seventy-five percent or more of a group using club facilities are members and payment is received from the members or their employers, then it is assumed that the non-members are guests of the members and not part of the general public. Thus the income is exempt.

But golf tournaments, where the participants are primarily non-members, are subject to the UBIT tax. The club can aggregate all of the non-member tournament income (such as greens fees, cart rentals, and sales of food and drink) and deduct the aggregate expenses in connection therewith in determining its UBIT. Further, non-traditional activities (such as catering outside the clubhouse or selling food or beverages for consumption off the club's premises) are generally considered unrelated business income. The Internal Revenue Service has twice ruled that income received from members of other clubs under reciprocal agreements is to be treated as income from non-members.

Clubs vary widely in their approach to handling income from initiation fees. Some clubs record these fees as part of operating income while other clubs consider such fees as contributions to capital, which adds to the member's equity. In the final analysis, such fees should be placed in the category where they are actually used. Some clubs (such as the Baltimore Country Club) use such fees exclusively for capital replacement and improvements, which is the recommendation of many club accountants.

The club may be required to pay tax on its investments unless the income is specifically set aside for charitable purposes. The gain from the sale of a clubhouse or other property used in direct performance of an exempt function will not be taxed if reinvested in replacement property beginning one year before the sale and ending three years after the sale. But if the gain is in excess of the price of the replacement property, the difference is subject to tax under Internal Revenue Code §512(a)(3)(D).

The following pages present a sample operating income for a hypothetical country club, together with the controller's comments.

Comments on April 2001 Operating Income (see table on next page)
by the Controller, Phyllis Whoo
Edited by the Treasurer, A. Justin Numbers

Overall
> The Operating Income for April of $65,826 was favorable to budget by $13,201. The Year-to-Date Operating Profit of $180,250 was favorable to budget, but was unfavorable to the prior year by $107,448.

Dues and Fees
> Revenue from Dues and Fees met or exceeded budget in all classes with an overall favorable variance of $19,500.

Guest & Cart &Other Fees
> Fees from Guest and Cart Fees, and other fee areas, were unfavorable by $3,000.

Food and Beverage
> Food and Beverage April volume again fell short of budget by $561. However, Operating Income was better than budget by $3,239.

> The labor cost increase is a continuation of what we saw in the first quarter and has been addressed with the General Manager, the Food & Beverage Manager, and the Chef.

Golf Services
> Golf Services Operating profit was only $175 unfavorable to

Takhomasak Country Club
April 2001 Operating Income
(excludes depreciation)

Dept.	MONTH			YEAR-TO-DATE			LAST YEAR ACTUAL	
	Actual	Budget	Variance*	Actual	Budget	Variance*	Month	YTD
Dues & Fees	$334,040	$317,545	$16,495	$1,333,143	$1,318,295	$14,848	$309,679	$1,272,512
Food Dept.	(12,675)	(12,200)	(475)	(81,573)	(73,555)	(8,018)	2,221	(26,394)
Beverage Dept.	11,666	14,430	(2,764)	44,321	49,030	(4,709)	14,647	40,029
Golf Services	(18,390)	(18,215)	(175)	(72,919)	(76,360)	3,441	(14,417)	(68,070)
Tennis Services	(10,659)	(9,220)	(1,439)	(45,498)	(41,715)	(3,783)	(8,277)	(40,992)
General & Admin.	(63,190)	(65,645)	2,355	(272,458)	273,215	757	(61,271)	(256,347)
Membership & Rcpt.	(6,516)	(10,415)	3,899	(24,278)	(42,860)	18,582	(6,193)	(38,506)
Repairs & Maint.	(14,464)	(13,550)	(914)	(65,390)	(58,215)	(7,175)	(13,483)	(59,597)
Housekeeping	(9,579)	(11,050)	1,471	(38,191)	(45,610)	7,419	(7,753)	(29,684)
Utilities	(11,794)	(10,530)	(1,264)	(42,605)	(37,300)	(5,305)	(9,215)	(38,019)
Landscape Contract	(5,756)	(5,475)	(281)	(24,716)	(19,900)	(4,816)	(4,340)	(17,464)
Golf Course Maint.	(126,858)	(123,150)	(3,708)	(529,584)	(523,900)	(5,684)	(98,012)	(449,771)
Profit from Operations	65,826	52,625	13,201	180,250	174,695	5,555	103,587	287,698

*Better (Worse)

budget for the month. Sales volume was good, but cost was a little high, with payroll and other expenses favorable to budget.

Tennis Services

Although merchandise sales were favorable to budget this month, most of the expense items were unfavorable, resulting in an unfavorable variance of $1,439 for April.

General & Admin.

The bottom line in G & A was favorable to budget this month by $2,355, resulting in a year-to-date favorable variance of $757.

Membership

Membership is favorable to budget, but is due to the timing of some of the expenses in literature and advertising.

Maintenance

Clubhouse repairs are running higher than budgeted and the month's variance to budget is unfavorable by $914.

Golf Course Maintenance

Mower repairs and supplies continue to be unfavorable to budget, although there are savings on other items, bringing the month to an unfavorable variance of $3,708.

Notes

- Inventories in the Golf Pro Shop decreased by $13,000 to $81,800. (This is still higher than last year's level at this time.)
- Accounts Receivable decreased by $30,000 to $334,000.
- Our operating cash position remains in line with expectations. ▲

How to Handle Complaints

One of the most difficult jobs of a board member is the disciplining of fellow club members. For a club to sustain its status and reputation, however, it is necessary that errant club members be held to comply with club rules.

Get It in Writing

From the frivolous, ridiculous, and inconsequential to the dangerous and crucial, how the board member handles complaints can have a direct impact on the well-being of the club and the happiness of the membership.

Board members receive casual complaints from their constituents all the time—on the first tee or the tennis courts, in the locker room or at the bar. "I brought my Uncle Louie to lunch yesterday at the club," you might hear from Member Joe, "and it was ten minutes before we had a drink." Several responses are possible here, including, "Hey, how did you get special status? It took me fifteen minutes to be served."

In fact, this approach may be perfectly adequate, but beware. Joe may have been embarrassed by the poor service he received in front of Uncle Louie, whom he has been trying to impress. Nothing is more infuriating to any member with a real complaint than the impression that he is being brushed off. In most cases, you will want to rely on those four little words on which elected officials ultimately all rely: "I'll look into it." A mention to the general manager may be appropriate, and he

> Four indispensable words in the board member's official vocabulary: "Put it in writing."

in turn may decide to send Joe a brief note of apology. Case closed.

But what if the complaint is more serious, or the tone in which it is delivered more adamant? Four more indispensable words in the board member's official vocabulary: "Put it in writing."

All serious complaints should be registered in writing and directed to the board or to the president or, in appropriate cases, to the general manager (with a copy to the board). In the process of putting a complaint to words on paper, many members will decide the matter is not as serious as it appeared at first and thus drop it. If the member actually does register the complaint in writing, his letter will provide the "testimony" the board needs to investigate the matter.

Most clubs have a small group of chronically discontented members who can be counted on to contribute regular letters of complaint, but even these should be handled according to established procedure. *Every written complaint requires a prompt written response,* even if that response is only, "Your letter of July 31 has been received and contents noted." If the matter warrants an investigation, this should be mentioned in the board's first response, with an approximate timetable for resolution.

Complaints involving unlawful behavior or any legally actionable offense should be referred at once to the club's attorney for his advice on how to handle them. In this category, you will want to include all complaints alleging conduct that might be interpreted as sexual harassment, a hot-button issue discussed more fully elsewhere in this chapter.

If the procedure at your club is to refer such matters first to the Legal Committee, leaving them the responsibility of passing the matter on to the attorney, it's a good idea for the board to have a mechanism by which it can monitor the disposition of these complaints.

A complaint about (or from) a staff person should be referred to the general manager for disposition according to the procedures set forth in the employee manual. If you don't have an employee manual, get one. (See "Bad Apples" section at the end of this chapter.)

Complaints *against* the general manager (or any other club employee under a written contract) are best handled by the club president with a request for clarification from the accused party, and if appropriate, a consultation with the club attorney.

All other complaints should be scheduled for consideration by the full board or the executive committee. (As noted in Chapter 7, any sensitive matter is best discussed in executive session, where minutes are not required.) In reviewing any written complaint, the board should consider the matter according to the following criteria:

- Is the complaint coherent? If not, ask the complainant for clarification. The board's letter should acknowledge that the board is unclear in its understanding of the complaint and ask for the complaint to be rephrased and clarified. The board should not rephrase the letter itself ("We wish to know if what you mean is . . ."), which serves to put words into the mouth of the complainer. It is his responsibility to articulate a specific objection or grievance.

- Does the complainant have an ax to grind? Does he have a history of protesting a particular club policy (or criticizing a particular person's conduct) that makes his motivations suspect? That alone does not disqualify the complaint from serious consideration but does require a more critical eye. It is useful for the board to undertake its deliberations with knowledge of the context from which the complaint emerges.

- Can the facts of the complaint be verified? Were there witnesses to the incidents provoking the complaint—in which case, they should be interviewed—or is it a "she says/he says" situation? Do the principal parties agree on the facts but differ on the interpretation?

- Does the complainant suggest the possible presence of a larger problem than the one addressed? If the member complains bitterly of ice crystals in the club's ice cream, maybe the problem is with the refrigeration equipment, or maybe a supplier is delivering inferior goods.

- What is the complainant actually asking for by way of resolu-

tion? If he is justifiably aggriev-
ed, will the member be satisfied
with a written apology from the
board and a promise that the
event will not recur or that the
policy will be changed? Or does
the complainant expect more
direct retribution, perhaps censure of another member or the
termination of a club employee?

> When charges against a member are serious, the board should be able to rely on well-drawn bylaws for a procedure that affords the accused due process.

The frequency of complaints by members against members isn't surprising, considering the intimate level on which they interact at the typical club. Most are trivial: a slow group of golfers refusing to let faster players play through, a tennis player who repeatedly fails to return the errant tennis ball on the other court, parking viola-tions. Most such complaints can be handled without rising to full-board level. The penalty is usually a letter of reprimand.

When charges against a member are serious, the board should be able to rely on well-drawn bylaws for a procedure that affords the accused due process. A concept that finds its roots in the Fifth Amendment to the United States Constitution, "due process" means that a person who is accused shall have: 1) the right to know in advance what the charges are; 2) the right to a hearing before impar-tial judges; and 3) the right to defend himself against the charges.

In a club setting, due process requires that a complaint involv-ing a serious charge against a member must spell out what the offense is and how it violates one or more of the club rules. In most clubs, the impartial judges are the club board, excluding those board members who may have an interest in the matter.

Under some club bylaws, a special disciplinary panel conducts the hearing and reports its recommendations to the board for final judgment. Whatever your bylaws specify by way of handling serious complaints, you must follow the specified procedures to the letter.

Due process guarantees "the accused" the opportunity to testi-fy personally in his own defense and to call witnesses, as he deems appropriate. He's even within his rights to be represented by coun-sel during the proceedings if the circumstances and potential penalties are severe enough to so warrant.

Discipline

One of the most difficult jobs of a board member is the disciplining of fellow club members. For a club to sustain its status and reputation, however, it is necessary that errant club members be held to comply with club rules.

The scope of punishment (usually spelled out in the club's bylaws) can extend from a verbal admonishment to outright dismissal from the club, with various stages in between, as suggested here.

A phone call: "Hi, Jim. This is Pat Murphy from the club board. A complaint has been made that you hit into the foursome ahead of you, narrowly missing one of the older members. Jim, this is just a warning and a reminder to avoid such behavior in the future."

A letter: "Dear Jim: It has been reported that you hit into a foursome ahead of you last Friday, slightly injuring Mary Smith. This is the second time in two months that such a complaint has been made. If this occurs again, Jim, severe consequences may follow."

A fine: "Dear Mr. Jones: After a hearing, at which you were present, the board has determined to fine you $100 for violating the club rule for conduct unbecoming to a member. Fighting in the club bar just cannot be tolerated and if it occurs again, a more severe penalty may be imposed. Until the $100 is paid to the club treasurer, your membership rights are suspended."

A suspension: "Dear Mr. Jones: After a full hearing last Tuesday, at which you and your attorney were present, the club board has determined that your conduct of May 21 warrants a suspension from the club for a period of thirty days, during which time you may not enter the club property. The rights of your family remain unimpaired. Your financial obligations to the club shall continue during the period of suspension."

An expulsion: "Dear Mr. Jones: At a hearing held last Tuesday, at which you and your attorney were present, the board has determined that your conduct of repeated drunkenness at the club bar has reached the point where we must terminate your membership. The board takes this action reluctantly, but your problems with alcohol are beyond what the club can bear. You have been repeatedly warned about this but to no avail. Therefore, your rights as a member of the club, together with the rights of your family, are hereby terminated immediately. You may

> Suspension or expulsion can have an impact on a member's reputation, possibly even on his livelihood, so judiciousness on the part of the board is paramount.

not enter the club property either as a member or as a guest. We are sorry to take this action, but the good order of the club demands it."

Suspension or expulsion can have an impact on a member's reputation, possibly even on his livelihood, so judiciousness on the part of the board is paramount. If the club is diligent in the investigation of the facts, follows club procedure, and affords the member due process, then the club has a qualified privilege against claims of libel (written statements) and slander (oral statements).

For a form of bylaw dealing with member discipline, see Article IX of the Model Bylaws in the Appendix. The rule distinguishes between minor infractions, which are dealt with summarily, and major infractions, which are dealt with more formally.

Bad Apples

It happens to almost every club at one time or another: An anonymous phone call or unsigned letter alerts the club to the possibility of illegal conduct—usually theft, embezzlement, or taking kickbacks—by an employee.

Before approaching the employee, the board and the general manager should have a strategy in place for dealing with the matter. Their first step should be to consult with the club attorney, who will advise, as I do, that the law puts limitations on how far the club can go in conducting an aggressive investigation.

Depending on the nature of the crime suspected, the employee's computer records, business travel reports, and telephone logs can be examined. Listening in on his telephone conversations can be tricky. Federal law makes it illegal to tap into any phone conversation where neither party consents. Laws in twelve states—including California, Maryland, and Florida—require the approvals of *all* parties to a conversation.

You're probably within your rights to search the employee's locker, *if* it's the club's lock that secures the space. If the employee uses his own lock, check with your lawyer to avoid violation of privacy statutes.

You may want to request that the employee take a polygraph test, but be forewarned that the Federal Polygraph Protection Act of 1988 severely restricts the use and admissibility of these tests.

It is pretty much the club's call whether or not to report the perceived misconduct to law-enforcement authorities. Generally, unless the club takes affirmative steps to cover up the misconduct, there is no *obligation* of disclosure. If the criminal activity is widespread and/or involves top management, however, a criminal investigation is likely inevitable.

Sexual Harassment

Any claim of sexual harassment can be a source of great embarrassment for the club and can result in litigation with substantial economic consequences.

Freedom from problems of a sexual nature is a protected right under the Civil Rights Act of 1967. While private clubs that elect to operate under Internal Revenue Code §501(c)(7) are exempt under that act, many state laws on sexual harassment make no exception for private clubs. In any case, prudent board members will see that their club follows the federal guidelines.

Two back-to-back decisions in 1998 by the U.S. Supreme Court have helped to clarify that there are two types of sexual harassment. The first is called "*quid pro quo* harassment": "You sleep with me and I will see that you get a promotion."

The second type is "hostile environment," where unwelcome verbal or physical behavior (if severe and pervasive enough) is considered discriminatory. A constant stream of dirty jokes, nude pictures, and unwelcome touching, even in fun, can create a hostile environment in which the complainant's work performance is affected. In a club setting, sexual harassment can fall into three classes.

1. Superior-subordinate: This poses the greatest risk to the club because the supervisor can be held to be the agent for the club. The club can be held liable for the supervisor's misconduct even if the club has no actual knowledge of it.
2. Between co-workers: The club can be held liable for sexual harassment about which it knew or *should have known*, if the circumstances are such as to have created a hostile work environment or otherwise altered the conditions of employment.
3. Of club employees by members or guests. Again, if not stopped after notice to the club, this also can produce liability.

It is important that your club adopt a strong policy prohibiting sexual harassment, communicate that policy to all employees (be sure that new employees get the message), and maintain an effective complaint procedure. A sample policy statement follows:

Club Policy on Sexual Harassment

Sexual harassment of an employee, member, or guest by an individual is deemed to be offensive, and unacceptable behavior will not be tolerated.

The club is committed to creating a workplace free of sexual harassment, including:

- Unwelcome sexual advances
- Requests for sexual favors
- Other verbal or physical conduct of a sexual nature when:
  - Submission to such conduct is either explicitly or implicitly made a term or condition of an individual's employment
  - Submission or rejection of such conduct is used as a basis for employment decisions affecting the individual
  - Such conduct has the purpose or effect of unreasonably interfering with an individual's work performance or creating an intimidating, hostile, or offensive work environment

Any employees (including employees after termination) who believe they have been sexually harassed or abused at work by anyone (including co-workers, supervisors, members, guests, or visitors) must promptly notify their superior or the general manager.

All complaints will be handled promptly and confidentially. Confidentiality will extend to both the charging party and the person accused of sexual harassment, as well as all documentation resulting from the investigation.

Club officials will investigate all charges and take the appropriate corrective action to remedy all violations of this policy, including disciplinary measures up to and including termination, when justified. (If a club official is involved in the charges, such club official shall not be involved in the investigation or determination of appropriate corrective action.)

Individuals who report harassment, or who are involved in the investigation of sexual harassment, will not be subject to reprisal or retaliation. Any retaliation shall be reported immediately, and the club will take appropriate action. ▲

▲   Part Three   ▲

Running the Place

The Care and Feeding of the General Manager

11

Handled properly, regular reviews of the general manager's performance provide a structured framework for a give-and-take dialogue on management issues. They may even prove to be a catalyst for a worthwhile review, perhaps a revision, of the board's goals for the club.

Should You Provide a Contract?

In the familial atmosphere of private clubs, many boards choose to dispense with written contracts for the GM and other key employees. In fact, slightly less than half of the clubs responding to a recent survey by the National Club Association use written contracts (the average term of which is 2.5 years).

I think that's a mistake. The absence of a written contract simply means that the oral contract between the parties prevails—and that can mean a "he says/she says" situation in any dispute over terms (more likely "he says/he says," but that's another matter).

A good written contract provides certainty of terms. It should spell out in detail the following:

- The GM's responsibilities and job description
- The period of employment
- The salary and benefits accruing to the GM
- The circumstances under which the board may terminate the GM's employment

An oral contract suggests a certain casualness, as though neither party were taking the matter of employment very seriously. A written contract, in which both parties have thought about the terms, written them down, and signed the document, has *gravitas*.

Let's be frank, though: If a manager wants to leave, he will, contract or no. Ever since involuntary servitude was abolished, that's been the nature of employee-employer relationships in the modern world.

Defining the Job

A good general manager is part host, part den-father, part restaurateur, part groundskeeper, part marketing manager, part diplomat, and all business. It is a big job, and a difficult one—all the more so because the general manager must do his work under constant scrutiny. In the corporate world, a chief operating officer may spend his workdays among his peers and staff, but at least he isn't surrounded by his shareholders, as the club manager is in the form of his members.

Further complicating the GM's job is the fact that clubs are notoriously poor in defining exactly what they expect of their chief operating officer (COO). I believe that many of the problems that emerge between the board and general manager can be averted if the GM works from a very specific job description.

Creating a job description is a nine-step process.

1. Begin with a sentence or two broadly defining the scope of the general manager's duties: "As Chief Operating Officer of the Takhomasak Club, the General Manager shall provide the overall administration of the Club, pursuant to the policies and directives adopted by the Board of Governors and within the general provisions of the Bylaws and Club Rules."

2. Now break the job down into its component parts, such as: "The General Manager shall devote full time and abilities to supervision and coordination of all aspects of the Club's activities; maintenance and improvement of all Club assets

and facilities; protection of those assets and facilities; super-vision of all employees; administration of the operating bud-get set by the Board; and such other duties as may be assigned by the Board or the President."

3. At this point, draw the dividing lines of authority by specify-ing for whom the GM works. "In all duties and functions, the General Manager serves at the pleasure of the Board and reports to the President (or, in his absence, the Vice President)."

4. It may be a good idea here to insert some clarification of the GM's role *vis-à-vis* the general membership, roughly as fol-lows: "While the General Manager shall communicate with Club members, committees, the Board, Club officers, and staff members as necessary to accomplish the goals and objectives of the Club, the General Manager works only under the direction of the President and the Board."

5. Then explain who works for the general manager. "The General Manager shall be responsible for: (a) hiring, super-vising, and terminating all club personnel, except department managers and the Controller, which require the advice and consent of the Board; (b) establishing specific personnel policies, hourly wages, compensation benefits programs, job descriptions, and personnel procedures under the broad guidance and general approval of the Board."

6. In many clubs, individual department managers have estab-lished such tight control over their areas of responsibility that the board may find it useful to further underscore the ulti-mate power of the GM:

> "The Assistant General Manager, Golf Course Superintendent, Head Golf Professional, Maintenance Manager, Clubhouse Manager, Director of Tennis, and all department managers shall report to the General Manager in a manner consistent with the lines of authority and respon-sibility illustrated in the club organizational chart.
>
> "The General Manager may delegate to any of

these department heads the responsibility for direct supervision of personnel within the department, i.e., hiring and firing, setting salaries and wages as budgeted, and determining work schedules. However, the General Manager remains the ultimate authority in all such matters.

"Each department manager shall report to the General Manager on all administrative, accounting, and financial matters, including payroll, purchasing procedures on approved budgeted items (both capital and operational), personnel procedures, and reporting requirements imposed by regulatory agencies."

7. Now explain the general manager's financial responsibility:

"The General Manager shall coordinate with the Treasurer, the Controller, the Finance Committee, and other appropriate committees in the preparation of the annual budget for submission to the Board.

"The General Manager shall use sound fiscal methods to achieve the budget objectives approved by the Board in the annual operating budget."

8. Finally, define what is expected of the general manager in terms of his interactions with the board:

"The General Manager shall attend meetings of the Board and its various committees as an *ex officio* member."

9. If you want to be especially specific, attach a list of performance goals to the job description. These may serve to prioritize the general manager's responsibilities, thereby helping him understand exactly what is expected of his service to the club. Goals might include:

- Foster member satisfaction
- Establish open and frequent communication with the board
- Follow budget directives without compromise of services

- Maintain a stable and productive workforce
- Ensure the integrity of the physical plant

It's probably a good idea to outline the chain of command with respect to the club's controller. While technically working under the general manager, the controller should report

> A Dun & Bradstreet survey of the corporate world once showed that doing evaluations was second only to firing employees as the part of their job that management disliked most.

concurrently directly to the board or its designees, most usually the club president and/or treasurer.

A prototype of a typical chain of command can be found on the following page.

Evaluations

The more specific the job description the easier it will be for the board to evaluate the GM's performance, an unpopular task that nonetheless must be done at least annually. Nobody likes doing job performance evaluations. A Dun & Bradstreet survey of the corporate world once showed that doing evaluations was second only to firing employees as the part of their job that management disliked most.

But performance appraisals are vital for many reasons beyond the obvious one of monitoring the GM's day-to-day effectiveness. Handled properly, they provide a structured framework for a give-and-take dialogue on management issues.

Regular performance reviews can be a safeguard against simmering dissatisfactions on the part of the board and/or its primary employee. They may even prove to be catalysts for a worthwhile review, perhaps a revision, of the board's goals for the club.

Employee-evaluation instruments are widely available from a number of sources, including The Club Managers Association of America. The CMAA's "Performance Evaluation Program for the General Manager/Chief Operating Officer" sets out a system for assessment in which the general manager's work is reviewed not

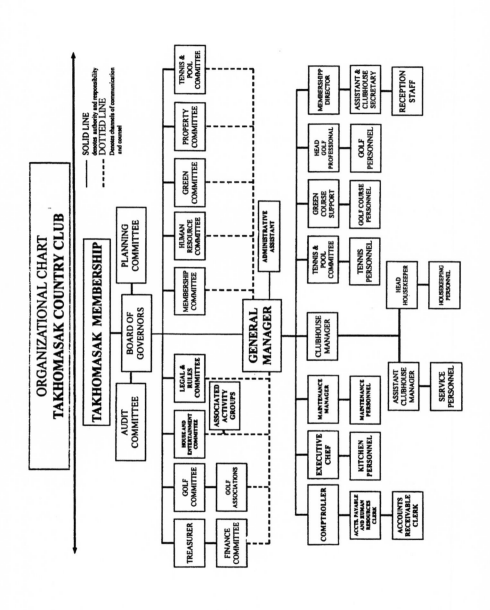

ORGANIZATIONAL CHART
TAKHOMASAK COUNTRY CLUB

TAKHOMASAK MEMBERSHIP

SOLID LINE
denotes authority and responsibility
DOTTED LINE
Denotes channels of communication
and counsel

only by the board but also by his subordinates, by club members, even by vendors with whom the GM has regular dealings.

The GM should be asked to evaluate his own performance by the same criteria offered to others, which can be an extremely revealing technique for determining whether the board and the general manager see the club, and his duties and performance, in precisely the same way.

> An annual review is an opportunity to assess not only the GM's performance in his job but also the nature of the job itself.

The CMAA's own performance-assessment program may be too detailed for your club's purposes, but it is worth your review as an excellent indicator of the kinds of feedback that a conscientious GM might hope to gain.

It is important to remember that performance reviews are conducted not only for the board's benefit but for the enlightenment of the general manager as well. His is an immensely complicated job, requiring that he serve, simultaneously, three distinct constituencies—the membership, the board, and the club staff—whose needs will sometimes conflict. An annual review is an opportunity to assess not only the GM's performance in his job but also the nature of the job itself.

Essentially, a performance review should break down according to the GM's trio of constituencies, beginning with the membership.

Are the members happy with the general manager?

There's no better way to answer this question than to ask the members directly, and each board member should have his trusted correspondents whom he can consult periodically for member input. But there are also several subjective indicators that should be observed, as follows:

- Is the general manager a conspicuous presence among the membership? Is his a familiar face in the restaurant and bar, on the golf course or tennis court, or does he seem to spend most of his time holed up in his office? When he's in his office, is the door open—literally and figuratively—for drop-in visits by the membership? Does he attend special events and make at least ceremonial appearances at private functions (birthday and anniversary parties, for example) held at the club? In everyday encounters, do members seem pleased to see the general manager? Do they greet him warmly, with an extended hand, or is there a frosty air of formality to their dining room hellos?

- How do the general manager and the members address one another? Every club has its idiosyncratic rules of protocol, but the Old World notion of the general manager as "Mr. Jones" rarely works in the "Hey, Frank" atmosphere of most American country clubs. Members are usually best served when they can relate to the general manager as a first-name peer. The general manager, on the other hand, should always address his members formally, as Mr. or Mrs.

- Does the GM make an effort to establish a personal relationship with his membership? In some larger clubs with inactive memberships, it may not be reasonable to expect him to recognize every face that comes in the door, but the general manager should certainly know his regulars by name. Does he remember their birthdays and anniversaries, inquire solicitously about their recent hospital stays, ask after their visiting granddaughters, compliment them on improvements in their golf scores? (This may be asking too much for even the best general manager.)

- Do members feel free to take their complaints and concerns directly to the general manager? As previously noted, most of the complaints that reach the board of directors will deal with what are essentially management issues. With patient effort, however, the board should be able to establish direct avenues of communication between the membership and the general manager, thereby lessening the volume of such complaints raised before the board.

- Is the general manager responsive to the concerns of his members? Once a complaint has reached him, either via the board or through direct interaction with the membership, is he effective in resolving the issue raised? Does he follow through quickly and consistently so that members feel that their concerns are important and their satisfaction is a top management priority? It is useful for the board as well to follow up on all complaints, both to underscore the importance of member satisfaction and to provide a means of judging the GM's performance in this crucial area.

Is the staff happy?

The best sort of performance review poses a list of specific questions to the board (and to the members and staff, if you wish to be that comprehensive) that call for quantifiable responses. To each question, each board member should be asked to respond according to a five-point numerical scale, with a score of 5 designating outstanding performance; 4 designating superior work; 3 for adequate; 2 for inadequate; and 1 for poor.

For an assessment of the general manager's performance as a staff supervisor, for example, the board may be asked the following:

- Is the GM able to maintain a stable workforce?
- Does employed staff function within budgetary guidelines, with no excessive reliance on costly overtime?
- Do employees seem content with their jobs?
- Does the GM delegate responsibility appropriately, or does he appear to micro-manage his staff?
- Is he effective in hiring, training, supervising, and terminating employees?

Note that certain of these questions deal with tangible indicators—high staff turnover may indicate a management problem of one kind or another—while others solicit the board's subjective assessments.

It is a bad idea to question the staff directly about the GM's work, unless that is understood to be part of your board's assessment routine. If staff opinions are to be part of your performance review, the general manager should know this when he is hired for the job, not discover it after the fact.

Is the board happy?

The final area of job performance to be considered solicits the board's subjective assessments of its own satisfaction with the general manager. Again, stick to questions that can be answered on a scale of 1 to 5, such as those suggested here:

- Does the general manager appear to be devoting the time necessary to do his job well?
- Does he regularly attend and actively participate in board and committee meetings?
- Does he provide complete, accurate, and timely reports to the board?
- Does he take direction well, without bridling at board involvement as an incursion onto his "turf"?
- Is he attentive to details of maintenance and improvement of club property and facilities?
- Does he display communication skills (speaking, writing, and listening) when dealing with the board, members, and staff?
- Does he exercise sound financial management and meet budget objectives?
- Does he willingly implement board policies and objectives?
- Does he show independence in speaking up when he disagrees with proposals?
- Does he maintain good personal appearance and display consistent courtesy on the job?

You may also want to include some questions that speak to the larger concerns of good management:

- Does your GM display qualities of leadership and vision?
- Is he a man of integrity?
- Has he shown creativity in proposing ideas and improving methods of doing things?

Evaluation forms should be distributed to board members well in advance. Set a deadline for the return of the completed forms. All assessment forms should be submitted anonymously, so that each board member feels free to speak his mind.

The easiest results to interpret are those that assign the GM a cumulative 1–5 ranking for each question, with annotations that include the range of his scores. (If your GM collects what appears to be a disproportionate number of 1's and 2's, even if his average is a 3, then it's worth investigating below the surface.)

Encourage members to contribute their own brief comments and observations, and include a sampling of these—point by point—in the preliminary report to the board. Make certain that the GM's strengths be acknowledged in equal measure to his weaknesses, by the way.

> The performance evaluation meeting should always be conducted by the president of the board.

Set aside adequate time at an executive session for general discussion of the survey results. The board should emerge from this meeting with a report on the GM's job performance, which is then conveyed to the general manager. A cover letter might summarize the results of the survey and propose a date for the formal evaluation.

The performance evaluation meeting should always be conducted by the president of the board (and the president's successor, if identified). At least one other board member should be present, but keep the group reasonably small so the GM doesn't feel overwhelmed.

It is important that the tone of the meeting be constructive. This is not a tutorial or an inquisition. The GM should be given the opportunity to discuss survey results and respond to criticisms. Be careful, though, how you solicit his responses. Do not make him feel that he has to defend himself.

How does he feel about this grade? Does he think he could have done better in that area? Some management specialists recommend conducting these evaluations by strictly separating the work from the person doing it. Never say, "You failed in this area." Say instead, "Your work was not up to standard."

Make sure to point out exceptional performance in the same way—not as "You did an excellent job in this task," but "Your work was excellent in this task." Do not shortchange the positive feedback your survey may contain. If the members love him, and the clubhouse has never looked better, and the staff has never been more attentive, this is the time to mention it. Too often, board members convey their praise to the general manager in casual remarks off the cuff and devote the performance evaluation only to what is wrong. A wise president, unless he has another agenda, will always end the review meeting on a positive note.

One way to conclude the performance review successfully is to turn the conversation toward the future:

- How can the general manager's goals be revised for the next employment period?
- Can deadlines be set for specific tasks?
- Do certain areas of concern deserve a special investigation by the GM, with a follow-up report to the board?

This might be a good place in the review to encourage the general manager to offer his views on how the board might be more effective in achieving club goals. You can be sure he will have some.

Once the review is completed, a report should be prepared and entered into the general manager's personnel file, along with the survey results and other evaluation indicators. These records will be a useful reference for performance evaluations later on and can be brought into discussion (by either side) during salary negotiations. Do not, though, enter into the club minutes the survey results or any discussions relating to them. These are confidential board matters.

According to statistics compiled by the Club Managers Association of America, the typical club changes its general manager every three or four years. Usually, the move is the GM's choice; he leaves for a better job at a better club. There's no reason, though, why your club can't keep a good GM a lot longer than the average.

It is the board's job to hire well and keep the best employees. That takes encouragement (even coddling), openness to the discussion of problems, patience, and the establishment of quantifiable and achievable goals. Remember that any shortcomings your general manager may have will be viewed by the membership as shortcomings of the board.

The Origins of Professional Club Management

Well into the twentieth century, country clubs were run like private estates, with little organized management. It was common for the board of the club to employ a cook and service workers for clubhouse chores. Later, a steward was employed to run the clubhouse. For the outdoors, the board hired a greenskeeper and maintenance staff. A golf professional—often English or Scottish by ancestry—was hired to teach the members the game of golf. (In some cases, these golf professionals later took over the management of their clubs.)

In some early clubs, certain affluent members would decide how much each member would have to "ante up" for the maintenance of club operations. This practice fell quickly out of favor following instatement of the federal income tax in 1916, after which even the very affluent became more conscious of how their money was spent. Thus began the era of professional club management.

The slow change in club management reflected changes going on as well in the business world. Centralization of management control in the hands of someone who does not have an ownership interest in the operation is a phenomenon of the last seventy-five years. Before that, the owners of a corporation were also the managers of the business. They may have called themselves a board, but they didn't bother with meetings and voting and the other trappings of board service today. The owners made decisions as they saw fit on all matters of policy and procedure. As Ralph D. Ward notes in his book *21st Century Corporate Board* (John D. Wiley & Sons, 1997), "The board was a legal device for legitimizing action already in the works, existing largely on paper to fill paperwork needs."

As businesses grew bigger and bigger, with ownership spread out among a larger and larger pool of shareholders, this old system became impractical. The notion evolved that there might be people who, by training or skill, could specialize in the management of businesses owned by others.

At first, these professional managers were strictly employees; their actions were answerable to a board on which they did not serve. Gradually, though, professional managers were placed on the boards of the businesses they served. Up until the 1950s, most corporate boards were dominated by management professionals who were employees of the company. During the 1980s and '90s, control shifted, and today "outside" directors of major corporations outnumber "inside" directors three to one.

In the club world, a general manager never serves on the board of governors for which he works. Nonetheless, club management is today dominated by individuals of considerable professional training. Many hold degrees in hospitality management, offered by more than two dozen schools, including such distinguished institutions as Cornell, Purdue, and Michigan State Universities.

In addition, the Club Managers Association of America offers its own accreditation program for members of the profession. For CMAA designation as a Certified Club Manager (CCM), the applicant must demonstrate his or her proficiency in accounting, computers, food and beverage management, purchasing, marketing, maintenance, environmental law, and personnel administration. Three hundred credits of education and/or service are required for certification.

CMAA also offers a Master Club Manager (MCM) designation in recognition of outstanding credentials. To qualify, a club manager must demonstrate a high standard of moral conduct, significant contribution to the profession, and a record of teaching and/or publishing on club issues. ▲

What To Do When a General Manager Isn't Working Out

12

Firing a general manager is so fraught with potential perils, legal and organizational, that the best advice anyone can give on the matter is: "Don't."

The Last Resort

Pop quiz: In which of the following situations is it appropriate for the board to fire a club's general manager?

- Although extremely popular with the membership he has served for fourteen years, the general manager chronically ignores board directives, comes late and unprepared to board meetings, and is often curt to the point of rudeness in his responses to board criticism.
- Although efficient, timely, and forthcoming in his dealings with the board, the general manager is unpopular with the membership, who judge him to be distant, preoccupied, and unresponsive to their complaints.
- Headstrong and independent-minded, the GM has clashed with a succession of clubhouse managers, causing instability in the kitchen and a decline in the quality of the food and service rendered.

> It's seldom easy to fire *anyone* anymore.

• The general manager has alienated both the golf pro and the chairman of the greens committee, causing a petition to be circulated among the golfing membership for his removal.

The clever student who answers "none of the above" advances to the head of the class and wins the Zen Prize for management in the modern era. After a hundred years of court decisions and legislative actions protecting workers from various forms of mistreatment, it's seldom easy to fire *anyone* anymore, and the more conspicuous the position and responsible the job, the more complicated termination becomes.

Firing a general manager is so fraught with potential perils, legal and organizational, that the best advice anyone can give on the matter is: "Don't." Except in extreme cases where the GM has committed some overtly criminal act—theft, falsification of records, assault—the prudent board will do everything it can to work the problem out.

Let's say that your general manager falls into the first of the categories designated above: the Autocrat. This is a GM who has been running the club pretty much his way for years, with little board interference. But your board is dealing with a long-standing problem that earlier boards did not address—precipitously declining membership, let's say—and you believe it's crucial that the GM and the board work closely together to map a strategy for the club's survival.

The GM feels that he's got better things to do, and his attitude shows it. He's rushed and impatient with the board, claiming that he's got too many pressing day-to-day duties to take time for strategy sessions, which are not part of his job description. The board, whose annual performance evaluations have consistently judged the GM to be inadequate in the area of his dealings with the board, feels that he is violating the clause in his contract that specifies he must take on any and all special assignments they may designate.

When the GM is once again thirty minutes late for a monthly board meeting, board member Johnson (who ran a prosperous, multinational corporation before his retirement and has an almost

The Gentle Way

My own experience in hiring bears out statistics compiled by the Club Managers Association of America: The typical manager stays at a club for four years on average and leaves on an amicable basis not because of any particular disagreement but simply for a better job.

There are numerous obvious advantages to keeping a manager in place well beyond the industry norm; a veteran GM can be an extremely valuable commodity to any club. He knows the territory, knows where the bodies are buried (so to speak), has a knowledge of the club's history and practices, knows the members and their preferences, has hired most of the staff, and has survived a number of boards and a number of board presidents.

With longevity, however, any employee may get a bit stale in the performance of his job, and inevitably the club may suffer from a resultant lack of vitality. Sometimes, even a capable manager must be encouraged to move on.

The gentle approach is best in these circumstances. Let the employee know in his annual performance review that his present contract may not be renewed, thus giving him adequate time to relocate. Be generous with severance pay and liberal in extending medical benefits beyond the period of employment. And indicate your willingness to provide a good reference. ▲

military impatience with insubordination) gets fed up and pushes his way into New Business to move that the GM be fired.

The first thing the board should do is get Mr. Johnson to withdraw the motion. Employee matters are never an appropriate subject for discussion on the public record. Reflecting in the minutes the board's dissatisfaction with the general manager might be used by the GM in a post-termination claim of slander, libel, or defamation of character. At the very least, notice in the minutes of the board's dissatisfaction will likely serve to rally supporters on both sides of the question, causing inevitable dissension among the membership and disrupting club harmony.

The decision to fire should never be made spontaneously, in the heat of the moment. Nor is it an action that should be railroaded through by an angry partisan with clout on the board. This is a board decision, arguably the most important board decision, and must be made only after cautious and well-reasoned deliberation. But it is essential that this action follow the application of what is called "progressive discipline."

The chair (or any other member of the board) can request that Mr. Johnson withdraw his motion so that the issue can be taken up in executive session. Neither a second nor a vote is required for withdrawal of a motion—just the agreement of the originating member—and no acknowledgment of the procedure need appear in the official minutes. As previously noted, minutes should be kept of the executive session but can be held as confidential for board use only. Keep in mind, however, that these minutes can be subpoenaed in the event that this matter ends up in court.

First Disciplinary Directive

Conversation in executive session should center on correction, not on termination. The board might draft a statement or resolution to the general manager explaining its dissatisfaction, as, for example: "It is the sense of the Board that the General Manager has repeatedly shown disregard for the Board's instructions, thereby creating a situation in which pressing institutional problems cannot be addressed in an efficient and timely manner."

This is no place for amorphous statements such as "The General Manager has displayed a bad attitude." Be specific. If the board's dissatisfactions have been addressed in the GM's annual performance reviews, mention it. Provide dates of the infractions at issue.

Rather than just listing grievances, make sure that your statement offers an explanation of why the board feels that the GM's behavior is detrimental to the club's well-being: "The Board believes the close cooperation of management to be essential for dealing effectively with the Club's declining membership."

Close with a request that the GM respond to the board statement in executive session following the next meeting. At that meeting, listen fairly to what he has to say. Is it possible that your schedule of board meetings conflicts with his job duties? Has the board been unrealistic in its demands for reports? Is the GM simply overworked?

> The progressive discipline approach may seem frustratingly drawn out, but it is important that the board be seen to give the recalcitrant GM every opportunity to correct his behavior.

Avoid introducing any punitive elements into the discussion. Your objective here is not to tell the general manager what will happen to him if he doesn't "shape up" but to come to some agreement with him, and among yourselves, on what the shape of his job reasonably might be.

Ideally, the board will conclude this meeting with at least the draft of a second statement to the GM, this time listing specific performance requirements and a timetable for the achievement of certain goals: "The Board hereby directs that the General Manager present a written, comprehensive review of the membership situation at the next board meeting [include the date], with no fewer than five suggestions for how the Club can reverse the current decline in its membership." Summarize the broad directives that emerge from the meeting, as, for example, "The Board restates its insistence that the GM attend monthly meetings punctually and remain in attendance until their adjournment."

Be comprehensive but judicious. Don't get bogged down in petty complaints: "The General Manager has several times left his car in the no-parking area outside the club entrance." And don't drop a whole duffel bag full of grievances in the GM's lap, which is itself a punitive act.

The Second Warning

If the general manager continues to ignore the board's specific directives, then the time has come to spell out the harsh consequences of his continued actions (or inaction, as the case may be).

An executive session of the board should compose a second letter, formally placing the GM on probation for a set period, during which he must complete specified tasks. The letter should clearly state that at the conclusion of this period—thirty days seems fair—the manager's performance will be reviewed once again, and the continuation of his service to the club will be put to a vote of the board.

The progressive discipline approach may seem frustratingly drawn out, but it is important that the board be seen to give the recalcitrant GM every opportunity to correct his behavior. In the event that he takes legal action for wrongful termination, the board must be seen to have been scrupulously fair in its handling of the matter. The membership, too, will expect assurances that the board did its best to avoid the disruption inherent in a change of management.

The board must always keep in mind that termination of a general manager, even a bad one, is unsettling for any club. Experienced club managers are not that easy to find and, once found, must be trained—a process that is likely to take longer than the sixty days a prudent board should give its GM to improve his performance.

If, finally, there seems no choice but to terminate the GM, the board vote to do so should be unanimous, if at all possible. Otherwise, dissenting directors may be called upon to testify on behalf of the discharged employee in any court action the GM may bring against the club. Whether the motion to discharge sets out specific predicating reasons depends on the nature of the GM's employment.

If the general manager is under a contract providing for a fixed term of service, termination before the end of that term can be done, liability-free, only "for cause." Some contracts spell out what may constitute "cause," but generally it is preferable to leave the phrase open to board interpretation. If you have documented your progressive dealings, you should be covered. It is incumbent upon the board to document the occasions on which the GM has failed to perform as contractually required.

When an employee does not have a contract, he is said to serve "at will." Absent any statutory or contractual provision to the contrary, "employment at will" laws (which prevail in such states as Florida, Indiana, and Pennsylvania) take for granted the power of either party to terminate an employment relationship for any reason. Or for no reason, since "employment at will" status technically frees both parties from having to explain their actions. First adopted in a Tennessee decision in 1884 (*Payne v. Western*), "employment at will" laws reflect the belief that the intimacy of the employer-employee relationship and the need for managerial discretion defy scrutiny by the courts.

As usual in the law, though, there are complications. The "employment at will" doctrine may be subject to certain statutory restrictions in your state, for example. And, if your club does not claim tax relief as a nonprofit organization, your hirings and firings may be subject to a range of stipulations under the Civil Rights Act of 1967. Most private clubs are exempt from the provisions of this act, but other laws may apply.

If a board truly wants to guarantee an unfettered "at will" relationship with any employee, it might consider inserting the following clause into the contract:

"I understand that my employment with the Takhomasak Club is entered into voluntarily and that I may resign at any time. Similarly, my employment may be terminated for any reason and at any time without previous notice."

Once the board has decided to terminate its general manager, the club's attorney should be consulted *before* the employee is notified. Provide your legal counsel with all the information you have relating to the matter: the GM's personnel file, his annual performance reviews, all correspondence that documents your attempts at progressive discipline. If there is a contract, provide him with a signed copy, even if your attorney was the individual who originally drew it up; he will need to reacquaint himself with the specifics of the agreement.

Provide him as well with the specifics of the severance package you intend to offer the GM. Give him time to search all these documents for red flags. And heed his advice. Careful vetting of a termination plan can save a club thousands of dollars and months of tumult.

The Severance Package
After your attorney has signed off on all the particulars of the

References

One of the touchy problems of a termination is the question of employee references. The club has no duty to warn a future employer but it cannot and should not (in a reference letter or in a phone call) mislead a future employer or misstate a fact that may be relied upon in a future hiring. On the other hand, if the club states facts that the terminated employee feels to be untrue, the employee may threaten to sue the club for libel (if written) or slander (if oral).

In any termination, the question of references will almost certainly arise, and the board should be prepared with a policy stating succinctly that references will not be provided for any employee who has been terminated. The club's employee manual should specify that if the employee leaves or is terminated the club will only supply information on the dates of employment and the position held. This policy should be consistently applied.

Explaining to a prospective employer why his previous boss will not provide a reference is the employee's problem, not the board's, and any concession the board may wish to make risks serious consequences.

Many states have laws that protect employers from legal action if they provide a negative report on a former employee, but those laws can be murky; a terminated employee with revenge on his mind can tie the club up in court and even exact financial reparations.

If, on the other hand, the club wishes to act generously by providing a positive reference for an employee it has had to fire, then the subsequent employer may one day hold your club responsible for the employee's misdeeds. (A 1997 ruling by the California Supreme Court found a school district negligent for providing a good reference for an employee who had been forced to resign because of allegations that he had sexually molested one of his students.) ▲

termination notice and severance package, it is time to present both to the employee. The board president is the person to do this, in the presence of one other board member who is there as a witness rather than as a participant.

Every effort should be made to preserve the GM's dignity. This is no time to laboriously review his inadequacies or to discuss in detail the decision the board has made. The meeting should be brief (fifteen to twenty minutes is sufficient), businesslike, and to the point. Here's one possible scenario, involving General Manager Sam Jones, Club President Jim Kindword, and Vice President Harry Aipe:

> "Sam, Harry and I have asked you in here to inform you of the board's decision to terminate your employment, effective at once."
>
> "What! I'm being fired just like that, with no notice?" (If progressive discipline has been administered properly, the decision to terminate him should come as no surprise to the general manager. Shock, though, is another matter.)
>
> "Sam, it was pointed out in your last performance review that the board was concerned by your failure to stay within your operating budget, your tendency to lose your temper with employees, and your failure to attend any of the significant social events of the year. At mid-year, you and I discussed these matters again, and I followed up with a memo to you requesting specific changes in your behavior. A month ago, you were placed on thirty-day probation, and still the board has seen no positive change. Our relationship, Sam, is hereby terminated."

At this point, the board president should outline the severance package agreed upon by the board and approved by legal counsel. Typically, the package includes payment of the GM's salary for a period of not less than thirty days. Unless there has been some blatant misconduct, I usually recommend sixty days, even longer for long-time managers—a generous gesture, perhaps, but one that sometimes forestalls legal action. (It's a good idea to make clear that the sum will be paid in the usual paycheck intervals, with the usual paycheck deductions.)

Additionally, the severance package should contain a dollars-and-cents explanation of the GM's vested interest, if any, in the club's retirement plan and a *written* statement of his health-insurance options under the Federal COBRA program. Under the Consolidated Omnibus Budget Reconciliation Act of 1985 (hence, COBRA), a terminated employee has the right to maintain, at his own expense, his membership in the employer's group-insurance plan for a period of eighteen months following termination. (Certain circumstances, including disability and divorce, can extend the time up to a total of thirty-six months.)

It is a good idea for the severance package to include an explanation of what the club's posture will be in the event that the terminated general manager decides to seek unemployment compensation. Any time a termination is "with cause," an employer may contest an employee's unemployment claim. But be prepared to accept the fact that most unemployment compensation hearings favor the employee and the proof has to be very strong in order for the state to deny compensation.

If the GM wishes to negotiate any of the financial terms of your settlement, this should be done at a later time and in writing. The club president should present only what the board has decided, and its attorney has approved. In exchange for these considerations, he will request that the GM sign an agreement specifying the following:

- That the terminated employee agrees not to file any suits or claims against the club, its board, officers, or staff relating to his employment or discharge. The proper wording, which your lawyer should frame, may be something like, "I, Sam Jones, hereby release the Takhomasak Country Club, its officers, directors, members, and employees from any and all claims, whether known or unknown, whether in tort or breach of contract or under state or federal law, pertaining to my employment at the Club or to the termination of my employment, or pertaining to any other matter relating to the released parties and myself." In signing this agreement, the employee says essentially that the matter is closed.

- That the terminated employee agrees to keep the terms of the agreement confidential.
- That the terminated employee agrees that the separation agreement was entered into voluntarily.

It is probably best that the GM be asked to remove his personal belongings from the premises immediately after the meeting. There is no point served in having him return to the club, possibly to rally dissension among the membership. Make sure that he turns in his keys, cell phone, and club credit cards.

In the event that the GM refuses to sign the agreement, of course, all payments to him (except his current paycheck) cease immediately until the matter is resolved. When any dispute arises regarding termination, consideration should be given to resolving the dispute by arbitration or mediation rather than litigation (with its resultant publicity and cost).

In mediation, the mediator serves as a facilitator, bringing both sides together to form their own agreement. In arbitration, on the other hand, the arbitrator imposes his own judgment on two parties unable to reach an agreement on their own. Arbitrated rulings are final, with no right of appeal (barring fraud).

In both instances, the parties involved pay for the service, but the results are usually a lot cheaper and quicker than a court proceeding—and a lot more private. Most states today have an established process for the certification of arbitrators and mediators. State bar association headquarters can give the names of certified arbitrators or mediators in the local area.

Once the meeting is concluded, the only task that remains is informing the membership, which should be done as soon as the GM has left the premises for the last time. Even though rumors will abound, the less said the better. Take care to word your termination agreement in such a way that board members can honestly say the decision was made "by mutual agreement," and that the terms of the agreement forbid either party from discussing it.

If you have a replacement GM standing by, announce his appointment in a conspicuously posted memo to the membership. If an employee is to fill in while the board considers candidates for the permanent job, announce that. By making Sam Jones's departure a secondary issue, the board acknowledges that it wishes old Sam nothing but the best in his search for "other opportunities," while stressing the opportunities that his departure provides for the club.

Sample Termination Agreement

This is an agreement between Sam Jones ("Jones") and Takhomasak Country Club Inc. ("Club").

The facts are that Jones has been an employee of the Club in the capacity of General Manager under a written contract dated June 5, 1999. The parties now desire to mutually terminate such written agreement and their relationship, on an amicable basis.

Now, therefore, the parties agree as follows:

1) By mutual agreement, Jones's employment with the Club shall terminate on May 1, 2002. On or before that date, he shall remove all his personal property from the Club premises, and shall deliver to the Club all credit cards, club keys, club-owned automobile, cellular phone, pager, computer, and any other Club property in his possession.

2) The written employment agreement dated June 5, 1999, is hereby terminated.

3) The Club shall continue Jones's salary for a period of eight weeks following termination, with the usual deductions heretofore taken.

4) The Club shall continue Jones and family on the Club's health benefit plan during the eight weeks following termination. Thereafter, Jones shall have all of the rights of a terminated employee allowed under the COBRA law.

5) All rights of Jones under the Club's H.R. 10 Pension Plan shall be deemed vested upon his termination, and he shall have such rights under the Plan as the Plan and the law afford.

6) If Jones is unemployed eight weeks following his termination, he shall have the right to apply for unemployment insurance benefits, and the Club will not oppose such application so long as Jones is in compliance with this Agreement.

7) Jones releases the Club, its officers, directors, members, and employees from any and all claims, whether known or unknown, whether in tort or breach of contract or under state or federal law, pertaining to his employment at the Club or in the termination of his employment, or pertaining to any other matter relating to the released parties and Jones.

8) Jones agrees not to take any Club employees with him to his new employment, nor will he encourage any employee of the Club to leave the Club's employment. To the extent he may legally do so, Jones will not allow any current employee of the Club to be employed by his new employer for a period of fourteen months from this date.

9) Jones agrees to keep confidential all matters pertaining to the Club that are not public knowledge as of the date hereof, including the terms of this Agreement.

10) The parties each agree that this Agreement is fair and reasonable to both parties and represents the entire agreement between the parties.

In witness whereof, the parties have signed this Agreement as of the 25th day of April, 2002.

How To Get the General Manager Your Club Deserves

No matter how dedicated the interim team, a club without a GM eventually begins to resemble an orchestra without a permanent conductor: things get sloppy and dissonant, and sooner or later the brass tries to dominate.

Take Your Time

Hiring a new general manager requires the full application of any club board's collective intelligence and skill. In this single stroke, after all, each member of the board has a chance to shape the club for years to come—maybe even to ensure its survival in the increasingly competitive marketplace for America's leisure time and dollars. No sensible board takes on the task of replacing its general manager without careful deliberation. But when it comes your way, there is no more satisfying experience in board service.

The wisely run club will have devised in advance a contingency plan for assigning the GM's responsibilities in the event that the top job is vacant. Some clubs opt for interim management. (The CMAA provides a list of retired club managers willing to take on short-term assignments.)

But even a best-case scenario imposes a heavy burden on the staff, club committees, and the board itself, all of whom will share in management chores. No matter how dedicated the interim team, a club without a GM eventually begins to resemble an orchestra without a permanent conductor: things get sloppy and dissonant, and sooner or later the brass tries to dominate.

> There is seldom a fast and easy way to hire a general manager.

The first thing a board must do is take a deep breath and face the fact that there is seldom a fast and easy way to hire a general manager. Unless providence puts the ideal candidate on your doorstep, 120 days is a likely timetable for the process. Ninety days will do, even sixty, if your club is lucky enough to have exceptional board members who can devote full time to the job. But typically four months is about right, one month each for the four principal stages:

1) Defining the job
2) Getting the word out
3) Identifying qualified candidates
4) Selecting the right person to fill the bill

Creating a Search Committee

The first step is to designate a committee to take charge of the search. Five members is an optimal number; the committee needs to be an odd number to avoid deadlock, but more than seven (heaven forbid!) gets unwieldy. The club president should serve on this panel, and perhaps two committee chairmen—probably House and Finance, which are typically the committees most closely involved in the operations of the club.

It's a good idea to reserve two slots for non-board members. In some respects, bringing in people from outside the administration of the club adds to the board's burden. Selecting these members requires its own search, and even the best choice inevitably will be a person who lacks the board's insider-understanding of club affairs.

You might want to fill the two general-member slots on your search panel with a past president and a *former* board member, thus ensuring that they too will possess a broad view of operations. By all means comb the membership for individuals whose professional backgrounds make them especially suited to the task. If you can find a member with experience in executive recruitment, for example, grab him. (If the outgoing general manager is going out under his own steam, incidentally, you might want to enlist his help but in an advisory capacity only. Don't let him control the process.)

The board itself should appoint the search-committee chairman, ideally someone from its own ranks. Not only is the chairman ultimately responsible for the deliberations and recommendations of his committee, he must also be able to express them to the board. A committee chairman who speaks the board's language—and knows all the idiosyncratic ins and outs of dealing with that body—will have an upper hand in keeping the hiring process moving forward. Then, too, chairing a search committee is a demanding and highly responsible job; it is appropriate that the person who takes it on be someone who is already sworn to protect the club's interests.

Once the committee and its chairman are in place, the board needs to set a budget and a schedule of deadlines. At the very least, expenses involved in hiring a new general manager will include advertising, background searches, and travel costs. The club will probably need to pay travel expenses for candidates the committee wishes to interview. There may be some relocation expenses involved. It is realistic to expect that a full search will likely cost the club between $7,000 and $15,000, possibly more.

With so substantial an investment, the board will reasonably expect regular reports on the progress of the committee and may require the opportunity to closely monitor its deliberations. It's a good idea to designate fixed deadlines for each stage of the process, with each deadline requiring a formal report to the full board.

In its first thirty days, for example, the search committee might be charged with reviewing what the club needs in a general manager, revising the GM's job description accordingly, determining basic qualifications, and proposing a plan for soliciting candidates. At the designated board meeting, the search committee comes prepared with the following:

- A written explanation of its rationale in determining what the club needs

- A full description of the duties of the general manager, such as appears in the previous chapter
- A briefer version of the GM's duties, such as might appear in a classified ad, with recommendations for where and how to post it

After discussion and any revision that may be deemed appropriate, the board votes to approve the committee's work thus far. The required margin for approval is up to you: two-thirds is okay; unanimous is better. If there's any disagreement now on what the GM job entails, there may be real trouble later on.

Then the board restates its agenda for the next report by the search committee: in another thirty days, the committee will have gotten the word out about the available position; thirty days after that, it will have isolated a batch of resumés to consider. (It's a good idea for the board to request that the committee supply a specific number of candidate resumés—no more than six.)

Defining What You Want in a General Manager

The conceptual work of defining the job is the part of the search process most likely to be shortchanged in the rush to get a warm body in the GM's chair.

But the first rule of shopping for anything is to know exactly what you want. In hiring a new chief of operations, a search committee must first take a hard look at what those operations are. In order to review both its short-term needs and its long-range goals, the committee must assess the present state of the club:

- Is membership slowly declining? Or rapidly aging?
- Has the club been successful in attracting a new generation of constituents?
- Are the facilities in need of modernization?
- Would it be able to survive increased competition, should it emerge?
- Based on a subjective reading of current indicators, where will the club be in five years? In ten?

Analysis of the club's current circumstances will dictate some of the specific skills the board will want to look for in a new GM. If operating costs have been claiming a greater and greater share of

> "The general manager should have VOICE," someone once summed up, meaning Vision, Organization, Intellect, Creativity, and Energy.

club income, for example, then the board should seek a candidate with a strong financial background and the demonstrated ability to hold the line against expenses. If maintaining membership is a problem, you'll want a GM with solid marketing experience.

For a membership riddled with Hatfields and McCoys, look for a diplomat who's had experience in navigating the treacherous waters of intra-club rivalries. Is there a major remodeling program coming up? Find a GM who has supervised a construction project. If the clubhouse restaurant is a problem area, look for a candidate with a strong food-and-beverage background.

Do you want a take-charge individual, a creative go-getter who's likely to come in and stir things up with change, or would the board and the membership be happier with a caretaker GM who will essentially maintain the status quo?

You will want to set a threshold of tangible qualifications: education, CMAA certification, and years of experience in the field. But don't be too rigid in these; you're not hiring a resumé. "The general manager should have VOICE," someone once summed up, meaning Vision, Organization, Intellect, Creativity, and Energy. If a candidate comes along with this powerful package of assets, you'd be shortsighted to pass him up solely because he lacks a degree in hospitality management. In hiring personnel, the intangibles are often what count the most. What kind of *person* do you want in the general manager's job?

And what exactly do you want him to do? Before beginning its search, the committee should create a job profile according to what it has identified as the current needs of the club. If the new GM will be expected to devise and manage a membership drive, say so. If the board expects the general manager to participate in club social functions, mention it. If there's been a history of control disputes between the GM and the groundskeeper, this is your chance to define the lines of authority once and for all.

Within reason, a job profile cannot be too explicit. The more specifics you can offer in advance, the less risk there will be of confusion and ill feelings later on. Rather than being daunted by a long list of duties and responsibilities, the kind of candidates you hope to attract will actually appreciate your efforts to help them see the job clearly.

But the principal beneficiary of all this detail is really the board itself. In discussing and approving the search committee's recommended job profile, the board will be forced to focus on its expectations for the new GM—which will be useful in determining an appropriate salary-and-benefits package, among other things.

Preparing a Classified Ad

Condensing the job profile into the parameters of a typical classified ad is another beneficial exercise in focus. Coming up with a description of the job in one hundred words or less will force the search committee to clarify its priorities—to decide what's essential and what's not. A hundred words isn't much, but that's about the maximum you can devote to a job description in an ad that also must identify the size and character of the club and outline the application procedure.

You may also want to specify the salary range in the ad. Some clubs prefer to hedge their bets with the all-purpose "Salary based on experience," or to put the burden of specifying a salary on the applicant himself ("Specify minimum salary required"). It will save both the search committee and the applicants considerable wasted time, however, if a salary range is specified at the outset.

Advertisements don't have to be quite so forthright about identifying the club. Name it if there's any reason to—if, for example, the national reputation of your club would be a significant draw for applicants—but otherwise there's something to be said for keeping your ads "blind." If you do identify the club, be sure to close your ad with those all-important three little words: "No calls, please."

So let's look at what we've got here:

> Large private country club in suburban Chicago seeks a
> take-charge general manager with a strong business
> background, willing to devote long hours toward build-

ing membership, improving services, and holding the line on costs. Physical plant includes an 18-hole golf course, 8 tennis courts, and a large clubhouse with a full bar, restaurant, and banquet facilities. GM supervises a staff of fifty and an annual budget of $4 million. Some college, ten years of work experience, and at least three years in a comparably responsible position required. Knowledge of food-and-beverage operations a must. Base salary $100,000, plus generous benefits. Send cover letter and resumé to the Chairman of the Search Committee at the following postbox address before November 15, 2001.

At 118 words, the ad is a little long. You might want to shorten up on the list of facilities (maybe "GM supervises a $25-million-dollar facility" says it all), or cut back the requirements to the one that's most important ("At least three years in a comparably responsible position required"). Classified ad rates are expensive in major-market newspapers, and you may be running your ad for weeks in multiple publications. Hold the ad to one hundred words at the absolute maximum.

Fifty words is probably a realistic minimum. It's possible to cut the above ad roughly in half as follows:

> Large private country club in suburban Chicago seeks a take-charge general manager to supervise a $25-million facility. Salary $100,000, plus generous benefits. Send cover letter and resumé to the Chairman of the Search Committee at the following postbox address before November 15, 2001.

It's up to the search committee to weigh the cost of advertising space versus the effectiveness of the ad. Generally speaking, though, the more specific the ad, the more likely it is that you will receive resumés from candidate whose backgrounds and skills are right on the money.

Once you know what you want, where do you look? The first place to advertise your search for a general manager is within the club—in the member newsletter or by conspicuous posting on the members' bulletin board. Your members will want to provide feedback and perhaps even make recommendations of candidates worth considering; it's in the board's best interest to involve the members as much as possible in the search. In one Florida club of my acquaintance, a club member recommended the GM of a Northern club for the top management job. Within two weeks, the candidate had traveled to Florida, been interviewed twice, and was offered the job. He turned out to be an excellent choice—sometimes you just get lucky.

> It's in the board's best interest to involve the members as much as possible in the search.

There may well be a worthy candidate within the present club staff, although that doesn't mean that the committee should end its search and take what's on hand. Hiring from within is a noble goal and can do wonders for employee morale, but you'll want to make your decision only after investigating the marketplace.

Cast a wide net. You'll almost certainly want to advertise in your local newspaper (and, as a result, be prepared to receive a resumé from every restaurant and hotel manager in town), but it is also a good idea to run your ad in the newspapers of major markets nearby. Have a look at trade magazines whose classified sections appeal to professionals in hospitality and/or recreational management.

In particular, you will want to consider *Club Management Magazine* (8730 Big Bend Blvd., St. Louis, MO 63119; 314-961-6644) and the newsletter of the National Club Association (One Lafayette Center, Washington, DC 20036; 202-822-9822). The alumni magazines of universities offering programs of study in the appropriate areas (Cornell, for example) are also a smart option.

It's usually free to post your ad with college and university employment bureaus. You will also want to be in touch with the Club Managers Association of America (1733 King Street, Alexandria, VA 22314; 703-739-9500). The CMAA's Executive Career Services Department maintains a job bank and distributes a weekly listing of openings in private clubs nationwide. This service is not free.

Every Friday, the CMAA publishes a Managerial Openings List (MOL) for subscribers. This MOL, which reaches a wide geographical area, is easy to use and reasonably priced. An ad of up to a half page of text (250–300 words) will cost about $500 for six weeks of publication.

If you want a narrower target, the CMAA will mail your very own Selective Search Bulletin to five hundred members within your geographic area for about $900—and you get a whole page for your message. Contact the organization for additional information and/or the appropriate forms. The CMAA also publishes an Executive Career Services Kit to help clubs make wise choices in a GM search.

Narrowing the Field

If the search committee doesn't generate a hundred resumés from its first advertisement for the job, something's wrong. The ad is too short or too narrowly focused or it's running in inappropriate media. If your ad is good, don't be surprised if your first responses number twice that.

The committee chairman (or his designee) should weed out the dross as the resumés arrive. Let's say that more than half of your one hundred respondents can be rejected out of hand—a reasonable expectation, in my experience. You'll want to eliminate sloppy resumés or those with conspicuous gaps. Get rid of the "jumpers" (those people who change jobs every two years or so), candidates whose careers are clearly on the way down rather than on the rise, and candidates whose qualifications do not meet the standards set by the search committee (the manager of a Burger King, for example).

Now someone must cut the list by roughly half again. The chairman can do this, but it doesn't hurt to enlist fresh eyes. Perhaps the chairman and the club president can work together to identify a core group of two dozen serious contenders. At this point, you may want to send a form letter to the candidates you have rejected. It's always a good idea to treat everyone with maximum courtesy, particularly if the club name appears in your advertisements. Say "Thank you for your resumé. Unfortunately, our needs and your qualifications do not mesh," or "Thank you for your resumé. We'll be in touch."

Ideally, each member of the search committee will have an opportunity to review all surviving resumés. Ask each reviewer to select the six most qualified candidates and rank them numerically. The individuals with the six highest cumulative scores are your semi-finalists. You will need to subject these candidates to a more thorough review, at the very least telephoning them for additional information or clarifications.

I think it's a good idea to ask each of these six to fill out a formal job application. Resumés are marketing tools, after all, wherein the candidate shows himself to his best advantage. With its unforgiving questions about references, the names of previous supervisors, and the circumstances under which the candidate left his previous jobs, a job application is more likely to reveal trouble spots. A job application provides you with the information you need to have rather than the information the candidate wants you to have.

A formal application also provides a legitimate way to obtain the candidate's Social Security number and home address, which you will need in order to run credit history and criminal background checks on him. Make sure the job application includes a clause, to be signed by the candidate, authorizing the club to investigate the candidate's professional, personal, educational, and credit histories. A second clause should ask the applicant to certify (with his signature) that all information provided in the application is true. Specify that false statements or omissions could be cause for refusal of employment or for dismissal once employment has commenced. If the candidate has made a major misstatement, you do not want him in your employ. (Remember the Latin phrase *Falsus in uno, falsus in omnibus*, which means roughly "A liar is a liar.")

Check all references. According to John Sibbald, president of an executive search firm specializing in recruiting top management for private clubs in *Club Management Magazine* (CMAA Conference Highlights Issue 2001, pp. 22, et seq.): "The best reference work is like . . . [the best] detective [work]. It is probing and often audacious. . . . Good reference checking is hard work. Lazy and superficial checking is worse than no checking at all."

Checking references can be legally risky unless a job candidate has expressly said you may do so. Should you ever disqualify a candidate because of information that has turned up in these third-party checks, do not mention this to the candidate, who may be able to make a case for defamation against someone who has given him a bad reference. (Keep in mind that one third of all defamation cases these days are employment-related.)

Once it has thoroughly vetted them, the search committee may want to conduct telephone interviews with its six semi-finalists. Then, the committee presents the names and resumés of the chosen ones to the full board at a designated meeting. If possible, this should be the only item on the agenda. You'll want to have plenty of time for unfettered discussion.

From these six names the board should select and approve three finalists, who will be invited to visit the club for an interview, and you'll want the vote to be unanimous, if possible. Candidates can be nominated and approved individually, of course, but it's a lot simpler if the pre-motion discussion isolates a slate of three to be designated simultaneously: "I move that the board contact Messrs. Jones, Smith, and Wesson to arrange for personal interviews with the search committee."

Permissible Investigation

Although the nonprofit status of many clubs exempts them from its provisions, the Equal Employment Opportunity Act of 1972 contains useful guidelines on what sorts of questions a prospective employer may ask a job candidate under the law. Later, in 1981, the EEOC set forth guidelines specifying the following:

Ask away:
> Name?
> Address (present and previous)?
> U.S. citizen?
> Educational background?
> Job history?
> Criminal convictions?
> Smoker?
> Drug user?

Don't ask:
> Age?

Married?
Children?
Nationality?
Health problems?
Race?
Religion?
Physical disabilities?

On the issue of drug use, note that it is permissible to ask a job candidate if he uses drugs. It is not permissible to request a drug test unless and until the job has been offered contingent upon the results of such a test. You also can't ask a job applicant to provide a photograph of himself, but if he does so voluntarily you're allowed to take a peek. Once you've offered him a job, you can require that he submit to a medical examination or provide proof of U.S. citizenship, a birth certificate, and educational transcripts.

Making the Choice

At this meeting, the full board might want to review the particulars of the interview process, which is fine. But beware if it appears that some members expect to become too much a part of it. Interviews are the search committee's job.

Schedule an informal reception with each candidate to which the full board is invited. It's best to schedule all three candidates for the same day. Assign each candidate a search committee host whose job it is to conduct a tour of the facility and in general make the visitor feel comfortable. Remember that the club is selling itself to the candidates as well. The best GM prospects may be sought after by more than one potential employer.

The club should be prepared to pay reasonable travel and lodging expenses for the candidates it elects to see in person. It's a good idea to introduce the search committee one or two members at a time, perhaps during the course of the facilities tour, so the candidate doesn't face the inevitably unsettling prospect of sitting down at a conference table with five complete strangers.

Choose a quiet space for the meeting, somewhere safe from interruptions. Try to keep the tone of the interview as relaxed and informal as possible but explain the ground rules that the committee has agreed upon in advance: "Our questions will take about an hour. After that, you will have some time to ask any questions you may have."

Before this meeting, the candidates should have received a packet of information about the club, including by-laws and financial statements, the job description and organizational chart, copies of the members' newsletter, perhaps historical background, maybe a club report on demographics, and an itinerary of the interview day. While some on the committee will want to ask questions designed to demonstrate that the candidate has done his homework on the club, remember that this is not a quiz. Nor should the interview be taken up with a review of credentials or other housekeeping details that should have been settled in the preliminaries.

What you're looking for here is some subjective measure of each candidate:

- How does he present himself?
- Is this a person who can work equally well with disparate constituencies? A club manager deals with people all day long—members, staff, vendors.
- Is he quick on his feet? Well-spoken? Does he look you in the eye?
- Does he have a sense of humor?
- Is he creative but deliberate? Playful but paternal? Charming but wise?

Whatever combination of ingredients you have in mind for a good general manager, can this guy fit the bill? Ultimately, all you've got is your instincts. Trust them.

Each candidate should be told when the board expects to reach a decision. Once the three interviews are concluded, the search committee might gather informally to discuss the long day—maybe over a well-earned drink (but not in the clubhouse bar). As a firm believer in the old saw that any decision is best made after a good night's sleep, I recommend that the committee select their choice for general manager the following day.

The search committee by now is essentially a jury, and like a jury it has been charged with a specific duty. Two months earlier, according to my schedule, the committee sought and received board endorsement of its ideal candidate. If you all agreed then that your club needs a hot-wire marketing specialist, you cannot justify hiring a candidate because he'd be fun to play golf with.

With voting, the simplest way seems as good as any to me: each committee member rates each finalist on a 1–3 scale, with the final nod going to the candidate with the highest number of points. If it's a two-way tie, eliminate the low man and vote again. If it's a three-way tie, well, God bless you—every club should have such problems. Unless, of course, the tie reflects a general dissatisfaction with the candidates proposed, in which case you need to start the process all over again.

When the voting is done, the committee must come to a consensus: "We agree that this is the person who fills our criteria for a General Manager." Hopefully, all committee members will sign on to the proposal.

When the committee has chosen a candidate to recommend for the job, it should do so formally, in writing, with the job description and the candidate's resumé and job application attached. At this point, after having made the selection of the three finalists and meeting each candidate, the board should have no trouble approving the committee's choice. Usually the club president makes the offering phone call. (There will still be some discussion of salary and benefits, but conduct those conversations in executive session. Discussion of compensation should never appear in the minutes.)

Hiring Help in the Search Process

For the board that simply lacks the time and/or resources to undertake the search for its own general manager, an executive search firm will do the job for a fee ranging upwards from 20 percent of the GM's first year's salary plus costs.

Some search firms are better than others, and some are very good indeed. In my own experience, the search is best conducted by the club itself, but if you need outside help, there are two sources you should contact first: the CMAA (703-739-9500) and the National Club Association (202-822-9822). Both organizations should be able to provide you with a list of several reputable companies that specialize in executive searches for the club industry. Stay with firms that are part of this industry. They have the knowledge—and the contacts—to do the job right.

Salary and Benefits

The club should resist any temptation to low-ball salary or benefits. That's the best way to ensure a short term for your new GM. According to statistics compiled by the National Club Association, club GM salaries range from a low of $80,000 per year to a high of $220,000, with the median slightly above $100,000. GMs who carry the designation "Chief Operating Officer" earn slightly more than those who don't. Predictably, big clubs pay more than small clubs, and city/athletic clubs pay substantially more than golf/country clubs.

In addition to salary, a benefits package might include one or more of the following:

- Retirement plan
- Full medical insurance (including prescription drugs, dental, and vision)
- Life insurance
- A leased automobile or car allowance
- Meals at the club (including spouse and family)
- Club privileges
- CMAA membership package (dues and expenses related to attendance at annual and regional meetings)
- Tuition reimbursement
- Dry cleaning allowance
- A bonus package for meeting preset goals

A majority of the clubs reporting to the National Club Association indicated that they give their GMs an annual bonus based on both objective and subjective criteria. Typically, bonuses ranged within 10 to 20 percent of base salary.

The GM's Job Description

A sample of a job description for the general manager of a country club, using the chief operating officer concept, is shown here. Although this job description is directed at a country club, the basic principles, duties, and job controls could be adapted to apply to most general manager club positions.

This document is intended to be a prototype form and should be used only after consultation with the club's attorney. The job description should be referenced in the general manager's employment contract.

I. Job Summary

The General Manager is the Chief Operating Officer of the Club and is responsible for the proper management of all aspects of the Club's activities to ensure maximum membership and general satisfaction; a sound financial operation compatible with the best interests of Members, their guests, and Club employees; the maintenance and improvement of the quality of the Club's services; and the security and protection of the Club's assets, facilities, and equipment. The General Manager implements policies established by the Board.

II. Job Controls

A. Supervision received

The General Manager shall report to the President (or in his absence the Vice President) and serves at the pleasure of the Board.

B. Supervision exercised

The Assistant General Manager, Golf Course Superintendent, Head Golf Professional, Maintenance Manager, Membership Director, Executive Secretary, and the Director of Tennis (department managers) shall report to the General Manager in a manner consistent with the lines of authority and responsibility illustrated in the Club Organizational Chart.

The Controller shall be under the supervision of the General Manager for employment and administrative matters but shall report on financial matters directly to the Board, the Finance Committee, and the Club officers.

The General Manager may elect to exercise varying degrees of employee supervision as a function of his position as Chief Operating Officer of the Club.

III. Major Duties
  A. The General Manager shall administer and manage all Club operations and shall devote full time and abilities exclusively to the operations of the Club and its facilities.
  B. The General Manager shall provide the overall administration of the Club pursuant to the policies and directives adopted by the Board and within the general provisions of the Club Bylaws and Club Rules.
  C. The General Manager shall be responsible for:
    1. The hiring, supervision, and termination of all Club personnel, except department managers and the Controller, which require the advice and consent of the Board;
    2. Establishing specific personnel policies, hourly wages, compensation benefits programs, job descriptions, and personnel procedures in coordination with standing committees and broad guidance and general approval of the Board.
  D. The General Manager shall coordinate the various operations, departments, and activities of the Club.
  E. The General Manager shall communicate with Club members, committees, the Board, Club officers, and staff members (as necessary) to accomplish the goals and objectives of the Club.
  F. The General Manager shall attend meetings of the Board and the various committees with respect to which he/she shall be designated an *ex officio* member.
  G. The General Manager shall:
    1. Coordinate the development of the Club's Strategic Plan.
    2. Establish, implement, and supervise personnel policies.
    3. Coordinate and develop operating and capital budgets and monitor monthly financial statements.
    4. Ensure that Club operations are in accordance with all applicable laws and regulations.
    5. Ensure the highest standards for the Club's food, beverage, recreation, and entertainment operations.
  H. Although the General Manager may delegate authority to the Clubhouse Manager, the Golf Course Superintendent, and all

sports professionals, the General Manager shall retain over-all responsibility for Club operations.

I. The General Manager shall use sound fiscal methods to achieve the budget objective approved by the Board in the annual operating budget. The General Manager shall coordinate with the Treasurer, the Finance Committee, and other appropriate committees in the preparation of the annual budget for submission to the Board.

J. The General Manager shall develop operational policies and is responsible for the creation and implementation of standard operating procedures for all areas of the Club. The General Manager shall coordinate all management functions of the Club.

K. The Golf Course Superintendent shall report to the General Manager on all administrative matters, accounting and financial, including payroll, purchasing procedures on approved budgeted items (both capital and operational), personnel procedures, and reporting requirements imposed by regulatory agencies. At his/her discretion, the General Manager may delegate to the Golf Course Superintendent responsibility for hiring and termination of his crew, salaries and wages as budgeted, and work schedules. The Golf Course Superintendent shall cooperate and coordinate with the Greens Committee Chairman on golf policy matters, course layout, and all other physical aspects of the golf course and grounds.

L. The General Manager shall discharge such other duties as may be assigned by the Board or the President.

▲ Part Four ▲

The Big Picture

Surveying the Membership

Employed judiciously, member surveys are an indispensable way for even the best board to fill in the blanks of its own knowledge.

The Importance of Feedback

Most of the feedback that any elected official receives from his constituency takes the form of complaint. Often those complaints are constructive, and the effective board member (or city councilman or congressman or president) will want to listen closely to the voices of the members he represents, no matter how difficult that sometimes may be.

But what of those members who have nothing to complain *about*—those who are perfectly happy with the club just the way it is? These are members who have full confidence in the board of directors to govern fairly and take action judiciously. While they may recognize some opportunities for improvement in the club's facilities, they know that these things take time. They may disagree with a particular club policy but accept that change will evolve at its own pace.

You will seldom hear a disparaging word about the club from

these members—the loyal core, the real source of every good club's strength. You will seldom hear a word from them at all, as a matter of fact, unless you make the first move.

The best tool for gauging your club's health, and monitoring your own performance as a board member, is the member survey. I strongly believe that every club should undertake a general survey of its membership *no less* than every five years. Every two years wouldn't hurt.

In our poll-happy age, opinion surveys are sometimes overused. Sometimes boards rely on surveys instead of voting their hearts and minds. An over-reliance on surveys can suggest a lack of confidence on the part of a club board. (I know one club that actually surveyed the membership on whether or not to repaper the ladies room.) It can also suggest that the board is just plain lazy; rather than thinking an issue through and arriving at a consensus on appropriate action, the board would rather put the burden on the membership whose interests it is sworn to represent.

Employed judiciously, however, member surveys are an indispensable way for even the best board to fill in the blanks of its own knowledge.

Short and Simple

Member surveys come in two types: "How are things going now?" and "What would you like in the future?" The first can help in:
- Testing solutions to club problems
- Evaluating club facilities and services
- Measuring member satisfaction in all club offerings
- Identifying non-essential club offerings
- Gauging the effectiveness of the board and club management
- Measuring member willingness to be assessed for capital improvements
- Testing member acceptance of major changes in club policy

For easier tabulation of results, you'll want to frame your questions so that they can be answered simply. Yes or no is as simple as it gets, but it won't get you a very satisfactory sense of nuance. I like questions that request a numerical rating: 1–5, most negative to most positive.

Sampling

Aside from questionnaires, usually sent out to all of the members, member reaction can be assessed using focus groups (discussed in Chapter 15) and by member sampling.

Sampling is a statistical method to make inferences about the entire membership from a representative sample. In other words, if a representative sample of ten percent of the membership shows that seventy percent would be agreeable to an assessment of $500 to redecorate the club's dining room, then we can infer that sixty to seventy percent of the membership would likewise agree. The board can go forward with planning for the redecoration and expect a majority to agree to the assessment when the written ballots are sent to the entire membership.

There are two major ways to sample: quota and random. In quota, an effort is made to reach a cross section of the membership by selected members based upon, say, age, club activity, gender, membership class, etc.

Random sampling is, well . . . random: every tenth name on the membership roster, for example. Most random sampling is done by telephone, using carefully worded questions. It is important that the number of questions be very limited. Some club members resent the intrusion, so handling the polling needs to be done delicately. The resentment should be kept at a minimum if there are only three or four questions calling for a yes or no answer.

All in all, a sampling survey is a troublesome way to solicit member opinions. If at all possible, a general survey is by far your best bet but sampling can provide quick answers to problems the board may have. ▲

In addition, though, make sure your questionnaire gives your members the space to express themselves in their own way—within, say, twenty words or so on any given subject. These member comments are a vital part of any survey, both in terms of the information they may provide and the good will they will engender among your members for the opportunity to make their points. You will find that some members will comment on *every* question.

Selecting and properly phrasing your survey's questions should be the responsibility of the survey committee chairman, under the guidance of the board. I suggest that the board make known at the outset any specific areas of concern it wants addressed (and any specific questions it wants repeated word-for-word, for comparative purposes, as discussed elsewhere). The survey committee then presents a proposed list of questions that the board can approve with a minimum of discussion and amendment.

If you have someone on the board or within the membership with professional experience in statistics and sampling, great—sign him up for committee service. There are also numerous books available on survey techniques that may help you design an effective questionnaire. But don't belabor the process; go with your instincts on what the club needs to know.

While a good survey should be comprehensive, it is axiomatic in the surveying profession that the greater the number of questions, the smaller the number of people who take the time to answer them. A survey of member satisfaction should be relatively short, roughly twenty questions.

In putting together your questionnaire, keep in mind that surveys are most useful if they not only measure prevailing opinions but also indicate how opinions have changed over time. Every survey you conduct should solicit responses that can be measured directly against the results of previous surveys. Even if you completely overhaul your survey instrument, try to retain some major questions from past years.

Although a survey questionnaire should always contain sufficient space for individual comments, tabulation and interpretation will be much easier if the questions are phrased to elicit uniform response, as in the following samples:

On a scale of 1 to 5 (with 1 indicating "very dissatisfied" and 5 indicating "very satisfied") how do you rate our golf course?

Greens	____
Fairways	____
Bunkers	____
Roughs	____
Cart paths	____
Tees	____

On a scale of 1 to 5, how do you rate club dining?

Speed of service	____
Staff appearance	____
Friendliness	____
Professionalism	____
Food quality	____
Food taste	____
Food presentation	____
Menu variety	____
Consistency	____

The Results Are In

Note that the issues posed here are simple, direct, and concisely worded. The more words and the more complicated the questions, the more opportunity there is for a member to misread the inquiry (and for the board to skew the questions toward the responses it hopes to receive).

Set a realistic deadline for returns and stick to it. I recommend asking that responses be returned within fourteen days. On the fifteenth day, the committee might begin telephoning the non-respondents to give them another five days. (A return envelope keyed to a number on the membership list, but not the member's club number, will tell you who responded.) At the end of three weeks, you should consider the survey closed.

No matter what pains a board goes through to prepare a useful and accessible survey instrument, not every member is going to respond. Don't take this personally; it's the nature of the beast. Six out of ten is a good response rate for a club survey, in my experience, with the higher response rate usually coming from the higher membership categories. Be careful about sending separate ques-

> There is no more direct expression of membership will than a general survey.

tionnaires to each half of a member couple, by the way. Often, only one member of a household will respond, thereby compromising your response rate.

If your response-rate falls below fifty percent, however, the survey results cannot be relied upon. Such a low response rate poses several important questions: Were the survey and accompanying letter properly phrased? Is the membership that lackadaisical about the club?

Another thing that can depress your response rate is a request that the respondents disclose their identity. Most members will feel freer to answer honestly if they do not have to sign their names. On the other hand, you will want to get as much information as you can about the people answering your questionnaire. A membership survey can be a means of generating vital demographic information, such as member age, gender, residence proximity, children, other club memberships, occupation, hobbies, and interests. (Do not ask about income level: Few will answer, some will lie, and many will resent the question.)

If the questions have been phrased well, tabulation of results should be straightforward. A committee of three to five tabulators should be able to do the recording and counting of the votes. To give credibility to the vote, the names of the tabulators should be published and each tabulator should sign the final count. When the results are posted, they should be over the names of the tabulators. A summary of the survey results should be prepared and placed in the club newsletter.

The board should have the first look at the survey results—and an opportunity to vote on declaring them official. Once official, the results should be entered into the minutes, thus ensuring their permanent place for future reference.

Post the results in a timely fashion. Wait too long and some will wonder if there's something in them the board wants to hide. You might want to give the members an opportunity to discuss the results with the board in a public forum of some kind. But make clear that this is not a voting session. Any action to be taken as a

Professional Help

Unless the club has people skilled in survey-taking, the board may want to seek professional assistance in survey preparation and implementation.

There are firms that specialize in doing surveys for private clubs. Fees are usually negotiable, but the service is typically quite expensive. Clubs that need the professional services the most are the least able to afford the cost of outside consultants.

According to survey consultants:
- They can identify areas that need to be surveyed.
- Their questions are better composed.
- Having the survey sent out by and returned to the consultant gives the survey more credibility.
- They have the ability to analyze the results and do some comparison with survey results in other clubs.
- They can get a higher member response than otherwise might be.

Where to find these miracle workers? The Club Managers Association and the National Club Association both keep lists of consultants. These lists are available to clubs. The magazine *Club Management*, which should be available from the General Manager, has ads for consultants. ▲

result of the survey should be directed by the board through its own deliberations.

And deliberate it should, for there is no more direct expression of membership will than a general survey. At the very least, results should shape the board's agenda for the remainder of its term of office. At best, it can provide a blueprint for action that may affect future boards for years to come. Remember, the results of a membership survey impose an obligation on the part of the board to act on member dissatisfaction expressed in the survey. ▲

Planning for the Future

A strategic plan provides a stable platform from which meaningful change can be launched within reasonable time parameters, and within the financial capacity of the club.

Competing in the Marketplace

These are truly the best of times and the worst of times for America's private clubs. Best, because clubs represent a flourishing $7 billion industry in this country, growing all the time. Worst, because competition is more and more intense for that huge chunk of discretionary spending.

For most clubs today, it's harder than ever to get members and harder to keep them. The penalties for not staying competitive can be severe. Even some of our most distinguished private clubs have lost ground in recent years, as proliferating options—newer clubs, better facilities, changes in social patterns—have drawn away essential new blood.

No club falters and fails overnight. Institutional vitality fades slowly, over many years, even generations. The board that presides over a club's decline is actually suffering the consequences of inaction by all the boards that came before. Every past board, every

past board member, shares responsibility for the long-range planning necessary to keep a club current. During
your term of office, you have become
part of that continuum. For all the
here-and-now issues you will deal with
as a member of the board, your highest

> A strategic plan implies
> change. Nobody needs
> a plan to maintain the
> status quo.

duty is to protect the *future* of the club. And you can't do that without a strategic plan.

I can hear the moans of protest from where I sit. Strategic plans
are the bane of the business world; isn't the point of club membership to get away from all that? Yes, it is—but as I indicated earlier, in some respects you ceased to be a club member when you
signed onto the board. You became a kind of guardian, sharing
responsibility for the club's success and for its future.

According to club-management guru William McMahon, no
modern club can achieve success—or remain successful—without a
strategic plan. It is, he says, no less than "the cornerstone for a successful club." And McMahon is equally precise about placing
responsibility on the board for devising and implementing the plan:
"If the board creates it, then the board will believe it."

But first the board has to agree on what a strategic plan *is*:

- A strategic plan implies change. Nobody needs a plan to
  maintain the status quo.
- A strategic plan is a structured outline of long-range goals,
  with step-by-step guidelines for how to achieve them.
- A strategic plan provides a stable platform from which meaningful change can be launched within reasonable time parameters, and within the financial capacity of the club.
- A strategic plan is a formal document, an official expression
  of the board's will. It should be adopted by at least a two-
  thirds majority of the board that originates it and subject to
  a vote of reaffirmation by each subsequent board that inher-
  its it.
- A strategic plan is fluid, constantly changing as realities shift
  and emerge, but at its core should exist a framework of fixed
  parameters defining the direction in which the club should

proceed over the course of a five-year period. (Five years is the average life expectancy for any strategic plan, but it still should be reviewed and appropriately revised on a yearly basis.)

- A strategic plan is specific. It is not enough that it set out a goal of "increased membership" or "improved facilities." A good plan will call for the addition of 150 members—or four new tennis courts—over the course of eighteen months, with a prescribed sequence of steps leading to that goal.
- A strategic plan is straightforward, easy to understand, and simple to implement. Its approach is pragmatic, nuts-and-bolts: if A, then B, then C.
- A strategic plan is intended to exploit opportunities as well as avert problems.
- A strategic plan poses practical solutions to objective realities.

Appointing an Ad Hoc Strategic Planning Committee

Some boards try to function as their own strategic planning unit, with the board itself devising the plan and supervising its implementation. In my experience, however, this adds too much to the typical board's already heavy burden. Better that a planning committee (with board representation) be established (under board supervision) to propose a strategic plan (for board approval).

I recommend a committee of eleven as sufficient to represent a genuine cross section of the membership. The choice of this committee is vital to the success of the strategic-planning effort. Take care to avoid including people who are resistant to change, but beware as well of the butterfly chasers, running off in all directions. A strategic plan is not a bunch of people sitting around a table saying, "what if?" Avoid non-conceptual thinkers, since planning implies working in the hypothetical. Choose people for their specific skills—someone with a background in statistical analysis, for example, or in market planning.

I think it's a good idea for the committee chairman to be drawn from the board, in order that there be a direct communication between the two bodies. There's no point in a committee's devising a plan that the board will not approve, so frequent consultation will be essential. Typically, the club president, general manager, and chief financial officer will serve as *ex officio* consultants to the committee. As I've suggested previously, former board members often make excellent candidates for committee service.

Do It Yourself or Call in a Pro?

One of the first decisions to be made after the board has committed itself to devising a strategic plan is whether to retain professional help with the process. If your club members do not have the time, the patience, the drive, and/or the leadership to do the work, then a professional planner can help—at a price.

While there are sophisticated techniques that an expert can bring to the process, consultants don't produce miracles. They have to work with what they're given. In some cases, a strategic-planning consultant will merely parrot back to a board or planning committee what it wants to hear. At the very least, however, *a consultant will get the job done,* which is more than can be said of many in-house planning committees that start out strong and quickly run out of steam.

For clubs desiring professional help in the strategic planning process, both the Club Managers Association of America (703-739-9500) and the National Club Association (202-822-9822) have lists of reliable consulting firms specializing in private clubs. Each organization's magazine (*Club Management* and *Club Director,* respectively) carries advertisements for these and other firms.

Telephone a few in or near your area and request both a brochure of services and a list of recent club clients. As with all references, check them. Once you have isolated two or three consultants whose references are in order, draft a letter outlining your needs, your timetable, and the availability of data. Ask each of your candidates to come by the club for a meeting with the board or its designees.

Following these in-person sessions, the consulting firms should be able to get back to you with a proposal that includes a detailed description of how they will go about devising your strategic plan, the names and backgrounds of the individuals with whom you will be working, a schedule of deadlines, and a bid. (As always, keep in mind that the lowest price does not necessarily mean the best choice.)

Once hired, the consulting team drives the process. They're the generals. They will schedule meetings and preside over most of them, help set the objectives and goals, devise the action-plan, and prepare the final planning document. The plan they devise should represent a consensus of the views of both the planning committee and the consultant, and should follow logically from the factual data assembled by the committee.

Devising and Implementing the Plan

Once the planning committee is set, the chairman should solicit its input in assigning tasks and responsibilities. The strategic-planning process breaks down into six general stages:

1. Organizing subcommittees to break up the work of developing the necessary underlying data
2. Conducting research
3. Compiling and analyzing the research data
4. Recommending objectives and defining goals
5. Devising a plan to achieve those goals
6. Approving the plan

The planning committee will be more productive—and produce a better plan—if its members can work in areas that interest them or in which they have some demonstrable skill.

Before the planning committee can begin its work, the board must establish

- A procedure for amending, adopting, and implementing the strategic plan
- A timetable
- A mechanism for its ongoing review

Six months is not too much time to devote to development of a full, multi-objective strategic plan. There's no reason why the board shouldn't be working toward one objective while the next is being refined.

Assembling the Facts

Strategic plans are fact-based instruments, which means that the planning committee's first step toward creating one must be assembling a foundation of information in three key areas: members, money, and the market.

A strategic plan should begin with a careful review of the membership rolls, which are to a private club roughly what sales records are to a business operation. At the very least, you will need to know the membership total at the end of each year (or multi-year period) of the club's history. If your club has been around an unusually long time, there's no need to delve back into the dark ages; hold your research to the post-war period. (That's World War II, by the way, not the Gulf War.)

Good records (and a little digging) will usually reveal the number of members who dropped out during any given year and the number of new members who joined. The best records will isolate valuable demographics for each year: median age of the existing membership, average age of new members, gender, marital status, income level, distance lived from the club, number of months a year spent elsewhere.

The next target is the club's financial records for the corresponding period.

- What were the revenues and operating expenses for each of the past ten years?
- How much was spent on capital improvements for each year?

You should be able to break down both categories into their components:

Income:

What percentage of each year's income was represented by
- Initiation fees
- Food-service, etc.

Expenses:

What percentage of expenses went to
- Food service
- Facilities maintenance
- Generation of new memberships

Market Conditions:

Now look outside the club for market conditions that may have affected its fortunes during the target period.

- What changes have taken place in the club's environment?
- Has the population grown, ebbed, gotten older or younger?
- Have there been shifts in the area's economic base?
- What are the competitive circumstances—are there new clubs in the area, or other purveyors of services similar to those offered by your club?
- Have lifestyles changed among your target population—are they looking these days for a club with a fitness center or a club offering a smoke-free environment?

Are there development projects (private or public) in the works that will have an impact on the region? Study census reports. Consult with the government planning council(s) in your area, business-development groups, major employers, realtors, regional movers-and-shakers—what's their take on how the area has changed during the life of the club, and what do they know (that you may not) about the future?

Once the fact-gathering part of the process has been completed, the committee needs to prepare graphs or charts showing trends, together with a narrative profile of what they have found, such as the following:

Membership grew steadily from its founding in 1964 until 1978, when the Takhomasak Club stood at the full 440-member strength permitted in the bylaws. In 1981, membership dipped for the first time below that of the previous year. From 1982 until 1984, membership declined almost 20 percent and then remained essentially flat for the next five years. Since 1992, membership has been decreasing at about 2 percent a year; the present total of 335 still stands well below the all-time peak reached in 1978.

A membership survey in 1968 revealed a median age of 54.8. The membership aged steadily until 1988, when it reached 66.2. Between that year and 1998, the median age declined incrementally to 64.1, roughly the level at which it now stands. Twenty percent of the membership is now single women, as opposed to 0 percent in 1964 and 9 percent in 1975. As the median age of male members (married or single) rose slightly from 1988 to the present, the decline in the total membership's median age is wholly attributable to the new female population.

Excepting 1983–1985, when income declined a total of 15 percent, gross income from operations has risen each year. The percentage of gross income necessary to cover operating expenses, however, has increased as well, from 77 percent in 1980, to 84 percent in 1990, to 87 percent in 1998. Because net income (after operating expenses) is used for elective maintenance projects, the amount of actual dollars expended for such projects has declined by one-third since 1980.

Since 1990, perhaps as a result of the drop in elective maintenance, the cost of mandatory maintenance has increased a full 20 percent. During the same period, a decline in new members has produced a comparable decline in the annual pool of initiation fees (from which capital improvements are financed). An urgently needed addition of four new tennis courts will wipe out virtually the entire balance remaining in the initiation fees/capital-improvements account.

The Club's market territory has changed significantly in the past ten years, during which period there has been an influx of computer-software operations into the area. The population of those living within a one-hundred-mile radius of the Club was sixty thousand in 1964, with a median age of 59.9. Today, following increased residential development to the west of the interstate highway, there are eighty-five thousand people living in the area, with a median age of 49.4.

While Takhomasak remains the only full-facility,

golf-and-tennis club within its geographic territory, a plethora of health clubs (four so far), tennis clubs (two), and public golf courses (two) has emerged in the past decade to serve the area's new population of young professionals.

This scaled-down sample reveals several possible objectives for Takhomasak's strategic plan. The club clearly needs to address its escalating cost-to-revenues ratio, for one thing, and it needs to devise a way to pay for those four new tennis courts without draining the capital-improvements reserve fund. But most of all, what it needs is new members. Thus, Goal One for the strategic plan: "Within eighteen months, the Club will achieve, and thereafter maintain, a full membership in each of its basic member categories, bringing total club membership to the 440 cap designated in the Bylaws."

Strategizing
For our purposes here, the word "goals" defines the final objectives that the club wishes to reach, and "strategies" indicates the means by which the goals are to be achieved.

In order to accomplish Goal One, then, we might isolate the following three strategies:
- Mobilize the board and membership behind the membership effort.
- Strengthen staff support for membership programs through the hiring of a membership director.
- Develop and implement targeted programs.

Each goal, though, demands its own plan of attack. Thus, our designated goals might be described as follows:
Strategy One:
Mobilize the Board and membership behind the membership effort.

    1) Within 10 days of the Strategic Plan's adoption, the Board will have established a membership committee.

    2) Within 15 days of its establishment, the Membership Committee will have devised an incentive plan for enlisting

the active involvement of the existing membership.

3) Within 20 days of its establishment, the Committee will have drafted a letter to the general membership, explaining the importance of the new-membership program, urging full support, and explaining the incentives.

4) Within 30 days of its establishment, the Committee will have devised a "tickler" program to keep the campaign active among the membership over the course of the next year.

Strategy Two:

Strengthen staff support for membership programs through the hiring of a Membership Director.

1) Within 10 days of the Strategic Plan's adoption, the board will have agreed on a job description and salary level for the Membership Director, and will have designated a Search Committee.

2) Within 30 days of its appointment, the Search Committee will have identified and presented to the full board three viable candidates for the position of Membership Director.

3) Within 30 days of his hiring, the Membership Director will have devised a campaign with targeted goals.

4) Within 45 days of his hiring, the Membership Director will have implemented the campaign.

5) Within 90 days, the Membership Director will have generated a minimum of 20 new members.

Strategy Three:

Develop and implement no fewer than nine targeted programs for membership development.

1) Within 30 days of his hiring, the Membership Director will have devised a campaign to recapture lapsed members, including incentives for their return.

2) Within 60 days, he will have in place a plan for soliciting new members among young professionals.

3) Within 90 days, he will have in place a plan for soliciting new members among single women.

4) Within 120 days, the Director will have outlined an additional six targeted campaigns and devised plans for implementing them.

See "Sample Goal and Action Plan" for an excerpt from a sample plan that details more fully the steps a club might take to achieve Goal One. Your plan can be as specific as time and energy allow. It is critical, however, that it set definite, quantifiable strategies to be met at designated intervals.

Sample Goal and Action Plan

Goal One:

Within twenty-four months, the Club shall attain and sustain a full membership of 400.

Strategy One: *Date to accomplish:* January 1, 2002.
- Revitalize the Membership Committee by naming as its chairman an energetic, sales-oriented individual from the board.

- Select a committee of twelve members, seven of them Active Members of the Club (two of whom shall be women), three Junior Members (one of whom shall be a woman), and two spouses.

Strategy Two: Date to accomplish: March 1, 2002.

- Hire a new Membership Director to coordinate all aspects of the new membership program. Included among the Director's duties:
  - Identifying potential members
  - Streamlining the admission process
  - Planning (and conducting) membership-development events
  - Creating promotional materials
  - Monitoring existing levels of member satisfaction

Strategy Three: Date to accomplish: March 1, 2002.

- Develop specific plans and strategies to attract Active and Junior Members. Active Members (who represent the highest financial return to the Club) should be primary target.

Each year the Club loses approximately ten percent of its membership to death, relocation, or other circumstances. In order to reach our goal, we must bring in sixty new Active Members in each of the next two years. Our target audience consists of three categories of prospects:

- Residents within a twenty-five-mile area who are not members of any club but are nonetheless active in the golf and tennis community
- New residents moving into the community who have been members of clubs elsewhere
- Children of Active Members and Past Members who are now old enough to join a club on their own

Strategy Four: Date to accomplish: June 1, 2002:

- Encourage Past Members to rejoin by waiving the initiation fee.
- Host monthly cocktail parties for Prospective Members and their spouses, urging Active Members to invite (and accompany) designated prospects.

- Initiate a Legacy Program, by which children of members can join for a substantially reduced price.
- Mail membership applications to all Active Members, with a note asking that they pass the forms on to an appropriate prospect.
- Reduce initiation fees for all New Members until the membership capacity is achieved.
- Invite local realtors to the Club for a visit and propose a system of rewards for those who bring new prospects into the Club.
- Reduce the initiation fee for Junior Members and allow time-payments.
- Construct a fitness center adjacent to the tennis facilities.
- Secure the names of potential Junior Members from present Junior Members, and devise a system of rewards for those who bring in prospects. ▲

Communications and Crisis Management

Club boards have come to recognize pro-active public relations as an essential tool in the modern world. Today, PR is to a private club roughly what advertising is to a consumer product: a means of building and/or maintaining a positive public profile—of establishing a "brand identity" that differentiates it in the marketplace.

Straight Talk

Whenever board election time comes around, many candidates push for "better club communications." Once elected, though, few board members actually follow through. Yet, the very nature of a private club dictates that the members (for whom the club exists, after all) need to know what's going on.

How (and how well) the club communicates with its various constituencies—the membership, the board, the staff, and the public—usually depends on the staff, under the supervision of the general manager. But the ultimate responsibility for good club communications rests with the board.

The board should see to it that the club communicates to its membership:

- Frequently
- In a timely fashion
- Clearly
- Consistently

The Club Newsletter

The most vital avenue of intra-club communications is the members' newsletter. You will want your newsletter to include:

- Information on upcoming events
- Reports on past events

The ultimate responsibility for good club communications rests with the board.

- Committee reports
- Announcements of changes in policy or procedure
- A club calendar

The more frequently you publish your newsletter, the more time-

The Digital Newsletter

Advances in desktop publishing software have made it possible for a club to produce its own newsletter in-house at a fraction of the cost involved in jobbing the project out.

Select the software that is appropriate to the nature of the publication. If you only need to produce a few hundred copies, Microsoft Publisher, for example, will allow you to prepare a professional-looking master that can be photocopied inexpensively. Microsoft Publisher and comparable programs offer a range of first-rate newsletter templates that your club can use to circumvent the need for a professional designer. The program also includes a useful file of clip art (including photographs) which you can use to give variety to your pages.

If you're distributing more than a few hundred copies and using photos and color, you're better off using the services of a professional printer. You can still save considerable expense by providing "camera-ready" copy printed out on reproduction-quality paper. (Artwork should be provided separately, with photocopies in place to indicate "position only.")

If you want to go really big time, you might invest

ly will be the information it contains—and therefore the more useful the newsletter. A four-page newsletter once a month is far better than sixteen pages every three months.

There are those who say that a club newsletter should have a "letters to the editor" section to allow dissidents to blow off steam. I don't agree. While the board should listen carefully to the voices of dissent, it has no obligation to broadcast them. Such letters tend only to widen the level of discontent among those who have never thought about the issue raised. A club is neither a debating society nor a Jeffersonian democracy; the newsletter should speak board policy.

If there is a difficult question to be resolved, however, the

$1,000 or so in the hardware and software you'll need to produce your newsletter in digital format for the printer. A professional graphics program, either PageMaker or Quark, will allow you to create pages that can be converted readily to the plates your printer will use on press. Few printers can work directly from Microsoft Publisher files, although the latest version of PageMaker will allow you to convert Publisher files into PageMaker.

If you want your newsletter to include photographs, you have several choices. You can leave space for them in your layout and provide them separately for the printer to process for publication. You can take the original photos to a service bureau such as Kinko's and have them "scanned" onto a disk. Or you can scan them yourself on a desktop scanner that will cost upwards of $100. Keep in mind, though, that providing your printer with a disk on which all newsletter elements are present and in position will require that you invest in what is called a "zip drive." This piece of add-on equipment, which costs upwards of $150, will compress complex files and load them onto special disks ($10 each, by the way) that your printer can decipher. ▲

newsletter can be a useful vehicle for posting a "Notice of Proposed Action," laying out what the board is proposing to do and asking for member comment. This procedure is used by the federal and state regulatory agencies in proposed rule-making. Letting members express themselves *before* action is taken avoids a lot of criticism later on.

Be honest about whether you need professional help in producing your newsletter—and budget enough money to pay the going rate. It's easy enough in most communities to find freelancers who will write, design, edit, and prepare your newsletter for rates ranging upwards from $25–$40 an hour.

Using the Web

Today, most club members are computer literate, at least to the extent of having access to the World Wide Web (www). So it is not surprising that many clubs are using a webpage to attract new members and to communicate with their membership.

An interactive webpage allows members to:
   • Make and check on tee times
   • See the monthly calendar of events
   • Make dining reservations
   • See a list of new members
   • Print out their monthly bills
   • Receive other club information

The costs associated with webpage design and maintenance are reasonable in today's market, but go the extra mile and make it attractive, useful, and current. A billboard posted a year ago has little value to the membership.

The Outside World

Well into the second half of the twentieth century, most private clubs followed the old maxim that ladies and gentlemen had their names in the paper only at the time of their birth, marriage, and death. Because publicity usually meant trouble of one kind or another, often in the area of membership practices, the board's job typically was not to court public attention but to avoid it.

With recent heightened competition for new members, however, club boards have come to recognize proactive public relations as an essential tool in the modern world. Today, PR is to a private club roughly what advertising is to a consumer product: a means of building and/or maintaining a positive public profile—of establishing a "brand identity" that differentiates it in the marketplace.

The Press Release

The most basic tool of public relations is the press release: an announcement to the media of some action or activity of interest to the general public. If your club is sponsoring a golf tournament supporting a charity that's open to the community, that's cause for a press release to your local newspaper, which will almost certainly post a notice in one or another of its community bulletin boards.

The art of public relations lies in turning that brief calendar listing into a feature story by, say, aligning the tournament with a local charity or bringing in a newsworthy guest of honor for the awards banquet. The basic press release is still essential, and it still conveys the nuts and bolts of essential information: the who, what, when, and where. But a skillful press release secondarily serves to reinforce the image of the club as a good community citizen, a place where interesting people gather—whatever the desired image may be.

It never hurts to cultivate individuals within the media who are sympathetic to your club, but be careful not to abuse these fortunate relationships. Contact the press only when you have actual news of legitimate interest to the public beyond your own membership. Nothing wears an editor's patience thinner than a constant barrage of "stop-the-presses" phone calls or requests for coverage of events that interest no one but their participants.

The Press Kit

In addition to regular press releases, which focus on a specific action or event, every club should produce and have available for distribution what is called a "press kit." The press kit contains the sort of background information a reporter or editor might need to supplement its coverage of club events, such as:
- A brief history of the club
- A description of its physical facilities

How to write a press release

"Attorney and author John L. Carroll [who] will speak on 'How to Write a Press Release' [what] at 8 P.M. on Tuesday, the 12th of Never [when] at the Takhomasak Club in Lincoln [where]."

Technically, that's all you need. It doesn't hurt to add a quote (from someone pertinent) in the second paragraph, thus adding the authority of someone else's words, but in this medium shorter is better. No press release should ever exceed a single typed, double-spaced page, meticulously proofread for errors in spelling and grammar.

Make sure to print your release on club letterhead, with the name of a contact person—usually the general manager or the chairman of the committee sponsoring the event—featured prominently at the top. If an editor wants more information, he's not going to dig around for it. Editors are busy people.

The standard format for a press release is a pyramid with the most important information at the top, usually in the first sentence. This information will then escape the editorial pruning that goes on in busy newsrooms. You will be forgiven for plugging the club if you do it at the very end of the release, where it doesn't get in the way. ▲

- A page of evidence of its community involvement
- Copies of favorable news coverage the club may have received elsewhere
- A copy of the membership brochure
- Brief biographies of its board of directors, noting those individuals who can speak with authority on any areas of expertise. (Media are always on the hunt for experts to quote on one subject or another.)

- Contact information (name, title, phone number, e-mail address, etc.)

I recommend revising the press kit and distributing it the same time every year—timed to a specific annual event, ideally one that demonstrates community involvement. Journalism is a high-turnover profession; the young man covering golf for your local paper may have no idea that your club even exists, let alone that your golf pro spends one Saturday a month giving free lessons to minority kids on a nearby public course.

In most cases, your club will be able to handle its PR needs in-house. As the person on the premises during business hours, the club's general manager is inevitably a club's chief public relations officer. While he should be encouraged—even expected—to contribute to PR strategy and policy, setting strategy and devising policy are the board's job.

Sometimes, as when membership is in steep decline or the club is demonstrably suffering from negative public perception, you might be well advised to seek the help of a professional. The names of PR firms that specialize in the private club industry are available through CMAA and NCA, although hiring a local PR person who knows the local media may be the best choice.

Alternative Media

The communications explosion (with which many members are familiar through their professional backgrounds) can be turned to club advantage by a savvy board.

Electronic mail (e-mail), for example, offers an easy way to supplement your newsletter by posting news of events on a weekly—even daily—basis. E-mail addresses for online members can be grouped together for a "universal" posting that allows you to type your message only once, push the appropriate button, and send it to your club's own universe. If you want a personal salutation for the standardized message, there are computer programs that will merge the salutation with the message. There is almost nothing modern electronics can't do.

Cable TV operations in every community are required by federal law to provide "public access" opportunities within their sub-

scriber territories. Retailers have been quick to exploit the availability of free airtime, with weekly half- or quarter-hour informa-
tional programs that tie in to their marketing goals.

Clubs, too, can sponsor their own public-access "talk shows"—
golf or tennis tips from the club pro, interviews with members who
can speak with authority on one subject or another, discussions of
common interest to the club and its community. Usually, you will
pay a fee for the use of the cable channel's broadcasting facilities
and equipment, but the airtime itself is free.

Crisis Management

In an age when high schools are places of mass murder, no one
needs to be reminded anymore to expect the unexpected. A disgruntled former greenskeeper shoots up a golf course. A group of
clubhouse waitresses alleges a pattern of sexual harassment and
demands a fortune in reparations. The presumably benign fertilizer compound the club has been using for years turns out to contain
a chemical that's killing all the fish in that beautiful little stream
behind the 16th fairway. Six clubwomen file a claim of sex discrimination because they cannot play golf on Saturday morning. These
things happen.

It makes good sense for every private club to have a policy in
place for dealing with crisis—a crisis being any situation in which
negative public attention threatens the club's well-being, even its
very livelihood.

Rule One

Begin with the understanding that if there is a problem within its
control that can be corrected, the club will fix it at once. No PR
wizard nor the most brilliant crisis-management policy can put
a positive spin on the failure to act if action can be taken.

Rule Two

Never allow anyone to respond off the cuff. In the event of crisis, the club board and management should draft a formal
statement on the matter, in consultation with the club attorney,
public-relations consultant, if any, and other advisors.

Rule Three

Tell the truth. Accept responsibility, if appropriate. This is not the same thing as admitting guilt, by the way, and it is precisely because of such fine-hair legal distinctions that the club attorney needs to be consulted. ▲

Afterword

Confessions of a Board Has-been

Any conscientious board member will wonder from time to time if he is doing his job well. The fact that you're willing to question yourself probably means that you are doing just fine, as a matter of fact. You think things through, look at both sides of an issue, and can put aside your ego when board service so demands. These are all excellent signs.

Once your term of service is over, there are two certain indicators of whether or not you have performed well. The first, ironically, is that you will be immediately relegated to the cool backwaters of former-director status. Current directors will not seek the benefit of your experience. Club members will no longer solicit your wisdom. Your telephone will not ring. You're history.

The suddenness of the descent from board member to has-been makes it a shock, but it's a good thing. It means that you have served effectively. Your actions were deliberate and intelligently considered. And you left behind a clear record of the deliberations by which you arrived at your decisions. Nobody needs to ask for clarification or explanation. You've left a history.

The other sure sign that you've done a good job is that you will miss it. Not right away, perhaps: I felt relieved for about a month after my last term of board service ended. I enjoyed having more free time. My golf game improved. (When asked how his two terms as president had affected his game, Dwight Eisenhower replied, "A lot more people beat me now.")

Eventually, though, I started feeling a little edgy along about the third Thursday of every month—board night. I missed wrestling over issues, helping to set policy, contributing tangibly to the club's strength and the satisfaction of its membership. And I missed being an insider, no question about it.

But most of all I missed the fellowship. With only a sparse handful of exceptions, all of the boards on which I've served have consisted of intelligent, collegial, well-motivated people. I never attended a board meeting where I didn't gain some piece of information about the world and how it works.

So let me close with a toast to all club board members everywhere—present, past, or has-beens like me. (Maybe I'll run again; you never know.)

Here's to the satisfactions of board membership, and to the sounds of good people striving toward a better way.

Here's to the easy laughter of colleagues who appreciate that good sense is even better when accompanied by a good sense of humor.

Here's to the fairness of democratic rules of governance, equally applied; to tolerance of individual differences; to celebration of individual strengths.

May your board come to order gracefully, and may you feel the joys of board service as I have felt them over the years.

And lastly, as an old Irish toast puts it, may you be in heaven half an hour before the devil knows you're dead.

Appendix

Model Bylaws for a Country Club Using Equity Memberships

Table of Contents

Equity Membership Contribution
Significant Other
Conflict Between Bylaws and Articles of Incorporation

Article XI. General
Amendments
Dissolution
Indemnification

Bylaws of
The Takhomasak Country Club, Inc.
(Fictional)

Article I: General
Section 1: Name and Principal Office
The name of this corporation is Takhomasak Country Club, Inc. (hereinafter called "Club"). It is a not-for-profit corporation organized under the laws of the State of Lincoln. Its principal office is 1200 Country Club Drive, Potawatomi, Lincoln, which is its registered office under state law.
Section 2: Purpose
The purpose of the Club is to own and operate a private country club for the social enjoyment, recreation, pleasure, and benefit of its members and their guests. No portion of the net earnings shall enure to any Member.
Section 3: Club Emblem and Corporate Seal
The Club may have an emblem or other logo of a style and design as approved by the Board of Governors. The Corporate Seal of the Club shall be in the possession of the Secretary and shall be affixed on such documents as shall be required by law.

Article II: Memberships
Section 1: Types of Memberships
The Club shall have three categories of Equity Memberships, namely: Full Equity Membership, Tennis Equity Membership, and Social Equity Membership, referred to collectively as "Equity Memberships."

The Equity Memberships are further divided into Single or Family Memberships. A Single Membership shall be used by a person who is not married.

All other memberships shall be Family Memberships and shall include the husband and wife and their unmarried children under the age of 23 who are (a) living at home, (b) attending school on a full-time basis, or (c) are full-time members of the Armed Forces of the United States.

The Club, at its discretion, may offer Family Memberships to an individual and his or her significant other, subject to such requirements as the Board may determine.

Single and Family Memberships shall have an identical Equity Membership Contribution and Initiation Fee, but the monthly dues shall be allocated as the Board shall direct.

Section 2: Number of Memberships

There shall be a maximum of 325 Full Equity Members, 50 Tennis Equity Members, and 75 Social Equity Members

Section 3: Member Privileges

3.1 A Full Equity Membership entitles the Member to use all of the facilities of the Club.

3.2. A Tennis Equity Membership entitles the Member to have use of the tennis, pool, fitness center, and social facilities of the Club.

3.3. A Social Equity Membership entitles the Member to use all of the social, fitness center, and pool facilities of the Club.

3.4. Compliance with Club Rules: All of the rights and privileges to use the facilities of the Club are subject to compliance with these Bylaws and Club Rules and all amendments thereto.

Section 4: Membership Application and Acceptance

4.1 All applications for membership shall be on the form designated by the Board and shall be signed by the applicant. Each application shall be accompanied by cash or check in the full amount of the Equity Membership Contribution being applied for, together with the applicable Initiation Fee, which payment shall not be deemed accepted unless the membership application is approved by the Board. The payment of the amount for the Equity Membership Contribution may be made in installments, plus interest, as determined by the Board.

4.2. Within 30 days after receiving the application for membership, the Board shall act upon the application. The Board shall only approve applicants of good moral character and reputation, and who are deemed compatible with present Members. If three or more Board Members vote against approval of the applicant, the application is disapproved. Prior to taking action on the application the Board may refer the application to the Membership Committee for its recommendation. If the Board fails to act within 30 days after receiving the application, the application shall be deemed approved.

4.3. Comments from Members with respect to prospective Members shall be privileged communications, and only the Board shall have access to such information, which shall be held in strict confidence.

Section 5: Membership Certificates

5.1. The Club shall furnish to each Member a membership certificate in a form approved by the Board. Such certificate shall state that it is subject to the Bylaws and Club Rules, and all amendments thereto. Any accepted Member who is paying the required Equity Membership Contribution on an installment basis shall receive the equity membership certificate when final payment has been made. Until such time, the Member shall be treated as a Member for all purposes except the right to vote on matters coming before the Membership.

5.2. Equity Membership certificates may be issued in the joint names of husband and wife. Upon the death of one joint owner, the certificate shall be owned by the surviving spouse. Upon presentation of a death certificate, a new certificate will be issued in the name of the surviving spouse.

5.3 Membership certificates are not redeemable or transferable and are merely evidence of having an Equity Membership. Upon termination of membership for any cause, such termination shall operate to authorize the Club Secretary to effectuate the redemption, cancellation, purchase, or sale of the membership of the terminating Member in accordance with these Bylaws.

Section 6: Upgrading or Downgrading of Membership

An Equity Membership may be changed to a higher or lower category, if and when available, upon written application made to the Board, subject to the following:

An application to a higher equity membership category may be made at any time, providing there is a vacancy in such membership category. As a condition for the upgrade, the Member shall pay the difference between the Equity Membership Contribution and Initiation Fees (then in effect) of the membership category applied for, and the Equity Membership Contribution and Initiation Fees (then in effect) of the Equity Membership category held by the Member.

An application to a lower Equity Membership category, if approved, shall become effective on the first day of the following year. There shall be no refund on amounts paid for the higher Equity Membership category.

Article III: Board of Governors

Section 1: Number and Qualifications

The management and administration of the Club is vested in a Board of Governors, herein called "Board," which shall consist of nine voting Club Members in good standing.

Section 2: Term of Office

A full term of office for a Board Member shall be three years. No Member shall be elected to serve more than two consecutive, three-year terms on the

Board. Terms of office shall be staggered so that each year there shall be three Board Member vacancies to be filled by the Membership. In addition, any Board vacancies for which an unexpired term remains shall be filled by the Membership.

Section 3: Nominating Committee

3.1 At a meeting of the Board, held not less than 90 days before the Annual Meeting of the Membership, the Board shall appoint a Nominating Committee consisting of five Members of the Club, one of whom may be a Member of the Board not up for election. The Board shall designate the chairperson of the committee.

3.2 The names of the members of the Nominating Committee shall be promptly posted on the Club Bulletin Board.

3.3. Members of the Nominating Committee shall serve until the next Annual Meeting of the Membership. The Board shall fill any vacancies in the Nominating Committee.

Section 4: Procedure for Nominations

4.1 Promptly after their appointment, the Nominating Committee shall post a notice on the Club Bulletin Board requesting Members who wish to serve on the Board to present their names and resumés to the Committee. The Committee may also solicit candidates for the Board.

4.2. No member of the Nominating Committee shall be nominated by the Committee as a candidate for election to the Board.

4.3 Not less than 45 days before the Annual Meeting of the Membership, the Nominating Committee shall nominate not less than two more than enough candidates to fill the vacancies on the Board, which names shall be posted on the Club Bulletin Board.

4.4. At least 30 days before the Annual Meeting of the Membership, not less than 20 Members in good standing may nominate additional persons to the Board and such nominations, upon certification of eligibility by the Club Secretary, shall also be promptly posted on the Club Bulletin Board. Thereafter all candidates shall be given equal publicity and prominence.

4.5. Election of Members of the Board shall be conducted in accordance with Article VI of these Bylaws.

Section 5: Meetings of the Board

5.1. Meetings: The Board shall hold not less than nine regular meetings each year at such times as the Board shall determine. Within 10 days following the Annual Meeting of the Membership, the Board shall hold its Annual Meeting, at which time the Board shall elect the officers of the Club to serve until the next annual meeting of the Board and until their successors are elected and qualified.

5.2. Quorum: A majority of the Members of the Board shall constitute a quorum for the transaction of business at meetings of the Board.

5.3. Action Without a Meeting: Any action that could be taken by the Board may be taken without a meeting if consent in writing setting forth the action to be taken is signed by all the Board Members. An electronic mail (e-mail) consent may be given, provided the Board Member promptly thereafter confirms the consent in writing to the Secretary. Such written consent shall be treated as part of the official minutes of the Board and shall have the effect of a unanimous vote.

5.4. Telephonic Meetings: Board Members may participate in meetings of the Board by means of a conference telephone by which all Board Members can hear each other at the same time, and participation by such means shall constitute presence in person at such meeting.

Section 6: Powers of the Board

6.1. General Powers: Subject to the provisions of state law, the Articles of Incorporation, and these Bylaws, the Board shall have all of the power and do all of the acts necessary, proper, and incidental in carrying out the purposes, objectives, and business of the Club excepting only those powers that are specifically reserved to the Membership in these Bylaws. The Board shall act only as a board and the individual members shall have no separate powers as such.

6.2. Special Powers and Duties: In addition to its general powers, the Board shall have the following special and specific powers and duties:

A. Elect the Officers of the Club.

B. Appoint Standing and Ad Hoc committees and determine their duties and responsibilities.

C. Fill vacancies on the Board until the next election of Board Members by the Club Membership.

D. Appoint, hire, employ, select, remove, or discharge employees of the Club and delegate such authority as is necessary for the proper operation and management of the Club.

E. Remove officers and committee members and Chairmen.

F. Adopt, publish, alter, amend, or repeal Club Rules governing the use of the Club and its facilities by Members and guests.

G. Initiate proposals for the amendment or repeal of Club Bylaws.

H. Interpret and apply the Bylaws and Club Rules and other Club policies.

I. Determine the amount of the Equity Membership Contribution and Initiation Fees in each membership category and change same, as may be required from time to time.

J. Determine the amount of dues, fees, and other charges to be made.

K. Resolve any ambiguity or inconsistency between any two or more portions of these Bylaws.

L. Approve or disapprove any applications for membership.

M. Enter into contracts as may be required to carry out the business of the Club.

N. Create an official Club Bulletin Board and post thereon all approved board meeting minutes.

O. Levy assessments to satisfy operating deficits up to a maximum of 10% of aggregate annual dues without a membership vote.

P. Exchange rights to use the Club's facilities with members of other Clubs.

Q. Borrow money by short-term loans not exceeding 12 months duration in an aggregate, of not more than 10% of annual dues.

R. Provide insurance coverage to protect the Club's physical assets, to protect the Club, its Officers, and Board Members against insurable loss, and to protect the Club against fidelity losses in the handling of its funds.

S. Discipline Members pursuant to Article IX of these Bylaws.

6.3 Limitation of Powers of the Board: The Board shall have power to assess the Membership for capital improvements in an amount no greater than 10% of the aggregate annual dues in any one year. Any assessments in excess thereof shall comply with Article VII, Section 5 of the Bylaws.

Section 7: Removal and Replacement of Board Members

7.1 The Board shall have the authority to remove a Board Member who is found to be neglectful or unable to perform duties of a Board Member by the affirmative vote of two-thirds of the full Board. A copy of the charges being made against a Board Member shall be given to the Member at least 10 days before the meeting at which the charges are to be considered, at which meeting the Member shall have an opportunity to be heard. The decision of the Board shall be final.

7.2 A Member of the Board who fails to attend 50% of the regular Board meetings in a 12-month period shall be deemed to have resigned from the Board.

7.3 Following the removal, resignation, or death of a Board Member, the Board shall fill the vacancy until the next election of Board Members by the Membership, at which time the Membership shall elect a Member to fill the remainder of the unexpired term.

Section 8: Compensation

No Board Member shall receive compensation for services to the Club but shall be entitled to reimbursement for expenses reasonably incurred in performing duties under these Bylaws.

Article IV: Officers

Section 1. Election and Term of Office

At the first meeting of the Board following the annual meeting of the Membership, the Board shall elect from the Board, to serve a term of one year and until their successors shall be elected and qualified, a President, a Vice President, a Secretary, and a Treasurer, and such other officers as the Board shall deem appropriate. No officer shall serve more than two consecutive terms in the same office.

Section 2: Duties of Office

A. The President shall:
1. Act as the Chairman of the Board and preside at all meetings of the Board and the Club Membership;
2. Serve as the Chief Executive Officer of the Club and cause the Bylaws and Club Rules to be enforced;
3. Call special meetings of the Board, in accordance with these Bylaws;
4. Sign all obligations, contracts, deeds, mortgages, debt obligations, and other instruments as approved by the Board;
5. Supervise the activities of the Club's General Manager in accordance with the policies set forth by the Board;
6. Serve as an ex-officio member of all committees of the Club, unless the Board directs otherwise.

B. The Vice President shall:
1. Perform such duties as shall be required by these Bylaws or assigned by the Board;
2. Exercise such powers and duties as may be assigned by the Board or delegated by the President.

C. The Secretary shall:
1. Keep minutes of all meetings of the Board and of the Membership;
2. Be responsible for giving all required notices of Board or Membership meetings;
3. Provide for the security of all the Club's legal and official records;
4. Be the keeper of the official seal of the Club and shall attach same to legal documents when required;
5. Perform such other duties as shall be entrusted by the Board

D. The Treasurer shall:
1. Be the Chief Financial Officer of the Club and oversee the collection and disbursement of all Club funds;
2. Keep, or cause to be kept, books of account and all financial records of the Club;
3. Prepare budgets and financial statements for Board, staff, and Club use, as requested by the Board;
4. See that all funds of the Club are deposited in accounts in the name of the Club, in banks approved by the Board;
5. Perform all of the duties generally associated with the office of

Treasurer and such other duties as shall be assigned by the Board;

6. Give surety bond in an amount fixed by the Board and paid by the Club.

Section 3: Removal from Office

Any officer may be removed from office with or without cause, by a two-thirds vote of the Members of the Board.

Section 4: General Manager

The General Manager shall be employed to manage the affairs of the Club, in accordance with the direction of the Board, acting through the Club President, who will exercise supervisory authority over the General Manager. The General Manager shall:

1. Be authorized to incur expenses and capital expenditures in accordance with approved budgets, or as directed by the Board;
2. Attend all meetings of the Board (excluding Executive Sessions);
3. Be an *ex officio* member of all Committees;
4. Make reports of affairs of the Club to the President, to the Board, and to the Club Membership as requested by the Board or the President.

Article V: Committees

Section 1: Standing Committees

Each year, the President, with the approval of the Board, shall designate the chairman and members of the following standing committees: Membership, House, Finance, Golf, Greens, Property, Tennis, Entertainment, Pool, and Legal Affairs. Such committee appointments shall expire at the end of the Board year.

The Membership Committee shall investigate all applications for membership and report its findings and recommendations to the Board. The committee shall advise and recommend such action as may be necessary to keep the membership numbers up to the maximum numbers allowed in each membership category, as set by the Board.

The House Committee shall advise the Board on all matters pertaining to the Clubhouse and the equipment, furnishings, and property therein. The committee shall advise on all food and beverage operations. The committee shall oversee the enforcement of the Club Rules pertaining to the Clubhouse and the activities therein.

The Finance Committee shall oversee the Club's finances, which shall include Club insurance and tax returns. The committee shall assist in the preparation of the annual operating budget and the capital budget. The committee shall also recommend to the Board the person or firm to do the annual audit. The committee will review the audit results and shall report its findings and recommendations to the Treasurer and to the Board.

The **Golf Committee** shall advise the Board on the work of the golf professionals, the operation of the golf shop, bag room, golf carts, the maintenance of members' golf handicaps, and the formulation and promulgation of local rules for Members and guests. The committee shall oversee the enforcement of Club Rules as pertain to the playing of golf. The committee shall assist in the scheduling and carrying out of golf events.

The **Greens Committee** shall advise the Board on the Golf Course Superintendent's operations and the maintenance of the golf course, roads, cart paths, equipment, and buildings. The committee shall oversee all construction, renovation, or repair of golf-related properties.

The **Property Committee** shall oversee all of the physical properties of the Club, except in matters reserved for the House, Greens, Tennis, and Pool Committees. It shall oversee all property boundaries and monitor taxation of Club property.

The **Tennis and Fitness Center Committee** shall advise the Board on all matters pertaining to the tennis and fitness center facilities and tennis and fitness center staff of the Club, the promulgation of the playing rules for members and guests, the fitness center rules, and the programming of tennis events. The committee shall oversee the enforcement of Club Rules as pertain to the playing of tennis, the tennis courts, and facilities.

The **Entertainment Committee** shall advise the Board on matters pertaining to social activities and entertainment of Members and guests. The Entertainment Committee (along with the House Committee) shall oversee the enforcement of the Club Rules pertaining to the Clubhouse and activities therein.

The **Pool Committee** shall advise the Board on matters pertaining to the Club swimming pool, equipment, adjacent areas, and pool staff; the promulgation of rules regarding the pool and adjacent areas; and the programming of pool events. The committee shall oversee the enforcement of the Club Rules relating to the swimming pool and adjacent areas.

The **Legal Affairs Committee** shall oversee the publication of these Bylaws and the Club Rules; issue opinions for the Board on the interpretation of these Bylaws and Club Rules; and assist in the drafting of any amendments thereto and generally advise on any matters of a legal nature pertaining to the Club. The committee shall also advise the Board relating to member discipline.

Section 2: Ad Hoc Committees

The President, subject to the approval of the Board, may appoint ad hoc committees with specific assignments. All ad hoc committee appointments shall expire at the end of the Board year, unless earlier terminated by the Board.

Section 3: Termination of Committee Membership

The appointment of a member of a committee may be terminated at any time by the President with the approval of the Board.

Section 4: Powers of Committees

Unless the Board specifically directs otherwise, all committees shall act as consultants and advisors to the Board and no committee member shall act independently of the committee to which assigned.

Article VI: Membership Meetings and Voting

Section 1: Annual Meeting

An annual meeting of the Members of the Club shall be held each year at the Clubhouse of the Club on the second Thursday of February at 7:00 P.M. The purpose of such annual meeting shall be for the receiving of reports of officers and others, to announce the election of Board Members, and to attend to such other business as may properly be brought before the meeting.

Section 2: Special Meetings

Special meetings of the Membership may be called: (1) by the President; (2) by a majority of the Members of the Board; or (3) by written request of not fewer than 50 Club Members entitled to vote, specifying the reason and purpose for such meeting. The President shall set a date for such meeting not more than 60 days following such request by the Members. Notice of any special meeting shall specify the time, place, and purpose of the meeting. No other business shall be conducted than that for which the meeting has been specifically convened to consider.

Section 3: Notices of Meetings

Written notice of the annual meeting or any special meeting of the Membership shall be given by mail to all voting Members at least 30 days before the called meeting. A copy of such notice shall be posted on the Club bulletin board at the time of mailing.

Section 4: Quorum

So long as written notice has been given, no quorum shall be necessary for any annual or special meeting.

Section 5: Rules for Meetings

All meetings of the Membership and of the Board shall be conducted in accordance with parliamentary rules and procedures as set forth in Sturgis's *Standard Code of Parliamentary Procedure* (Third Edition), except as they conflict with these Bylaws.

Section 6: Voting by the Membership

All voting by the Membership shall be by written ballot mailed to the Members not less than 30 days prior to the date set for ballots to be in. In the case of ballots for election of Members of the Board of Governors, ballots shall be returned on or before 9:00 P.M. on the Friday before the date set for the annual meeting of the Membership.

Section 7: Allocation of Votes

Each Membership in good standing, whether in one or more names, is entitled to a single ballot. Votes shall be weighted by membership categories, based on the annual dues assigned for each category (rounded up or down to the nearest hundred dollars and factored down by the lowest common number for all categories). Example using Family Memberships:

	Full	Tennis	Social
Current dues	$3,040	$1,470	$1,045
Round (up or down)	3,000	1,500	1,000
Factor down (by 500)	6	3	2
Weighted Vote Value	6	3	2

Votes for Single Memberships shall be adjusted accordingly.

Section 8: Election of Board of Governors

In the voting for Members of the Board of Governors, those candidates receiving the highest number of weighted votes shall be declared elected for the full term of three years. The candidate receiving the next highest number of weighted votes shall be declared elected for any unexpired term of office being filled by the election.

Section 9: General

There shall be no cumulative voting and no preemptive rights. The results of all voting shall be promptly posted on the Club Bulletin Board.

Article VII: Fiscal Matters

Section 1: Equity Membership Contribution

Persons desiring to become members of the Club shall be required to make an Equity Membership Contribution in an amount to be determined by the Board. The Board shall have authority to offer deferred payment options for payment of the Equity Membership Contribution. A person acquiring a membership through a deferred payment option shall be entitled to all of the rights and subject to all of the membership obligations except the right to vote. Failure to pay any installment of the deferred membership contribution within 60 days following the due date will result in the forfeiture of the membership and all amounts previously paid.

Section 2: Initiation Fee

In addition to the Equity Membership Contribution, each new Member shall pay an Initiation Fee in an amount set by the Board. Initiation Fees shall be used for capital expenditures or repair and replacement of club facilities. The Board shall have authority to offer deferred payment options for the Initiation Fee.

Section 3: Club Fiscal Year

The Club shall conduct its financial affairs on a calendar year basis.

Section 4: Dues and Fees

4.1 No later than November 15 of each year the Board shall set the amount of dues and fees for the coming calendar year, which schedule of dues and fees shall be promptly posted on the club bulletin board. Fees shall include, but not be limited to, greens fees, cart rental fees, trail fees for members using their own carts, tennis court fees, locker rental, guest fees, and food and beverage minimums.

4.2 Dues shall be set in amounts projected to cover the Club's operating costs for the forthcoming calendar year together with reasonable reserves for repair and replacement of all improvements of the Club, plus a reasonable amount for new capital improvements.

4.3 All dues and fees shall be payable on a yearly basis and shall be paid within 30 days of the commencement of the calendar year. Members may elect to pay such dues and fees in equal monthly installments, without interest.

4.4 All three classes of membership shall be further divided into Family and Single Memberships. Dues and fees may vary within classes of membership, based upon Family or Single Memberships.

4.5 New Members shall pay dues and assessments prorated for the number of months remaining in the year.

Section 5: Assessments and Loans

5.1 The Board shall have the right to assess the Membership in amounts in excess of amounts provided in Article III, Section 6.3 of these Bylaws, only if approved by a vote of two-thirds of the Members of the Board and a majority of the weighted votes of the Members voting on such assessment, in accordance with voting procedures set forth elsewhere in these Bylaws.

5.2 Any borrowing, other than that authorized under Article III, Section 6.2 of these Bylaws, shall be approved by not less than a two-thirds vote of the Members of the Board and a majority of the Members voting on such loan (or loans) in accordance with the voting procedures set forth in Article VI of these Bylaws.

Section 6: Payment of Accounts

6.1 An itemized statement of account shall be mailed to each Member monthly. Any member failing to pay such monthly statement within thirty days of the statement date shall be charged a late payment fee or finance charge in the amount set by the Board, but not to exceed the maximum permitted by law. If such statement is not paid within sixty days of the statement date the Board shall have the right to have the Member's name posted on the Club Bulletin Board showing such delinquency. Thereafter, upon prior notice to the delinquent Member, the Club shall have the right to suspend all membership privileges until all past due accounts are paid in full. If the account continues to remain unpaid the Club shall have the right, after giving the delinquent Member fifteen days' written notice of the proposed action, to expel the Member and sue for the entire balance of the account, plus interest and attorneys' fees, to the extent permitted by law.

6.2 The Club shall have a lien against each Membership for any amounts unpaid, owed to the Club by the Member, which lien shall cover reasonable attorneys' fees incurred by the Club in the enforcement of the lien, whether or not legal proceedings are commenced to foreclose the lien. The lien may be recorded by the Club in the public records of the county and the lien shall remain in effect until all sums secured thereby are paid. The Club may foreclose such lien in the manner prescribed by law. The Club shall have the right of offset of any monies due the Member or former Member.

Section 7: Certified Audit

The Board shall provide for a certified audit of the books and records of the Club on an annual basis by a Certified Public Accountant or firm. Such audit report shall be available to the Membership for their review.

Article VIII: Termination of Membership

Section 1: Resignation of Membership

1.1. Any member of the Club may resign by giving written notice to the Club Secretary. If the notice of resignation is received by the Club on or before the fifth day of the month, the resignation shall be effective at the end of the month. If the notice of resignation is received after the fifth day of the month, the resignation shall become effective on the last day of the month succeeding the month of receipt.

1.2. Equity Memberships are not assignable or transferable except upon assignment to the Club under the terms and conditions set forth in this Article.

1.3. The Club shall be obligated to purchase the Equity Membership of a resigning Member only if an individual, who is acceptable to the Club, acquires an Equity Membership in the same membership category. The amount to be paid shall be the lesser of 90% of the amount of Equity Membership Contribution being paid for the membership by the new Member, or 90% of the Equity Membership Contribution made by the retiring Member, less any amounts owed to the Club by the resigning Member. The differential between the amount paid to the retiring Member and the amount paid by the new, replacement Member shall be placed in a special Member's Capital Fund to be used, at the discretion of the Board, for the repurchase of memberships prior to another individual acquiring a membership of the resigned Member. Any such purchase shall be from the oldest membership waiting on the list for repurchase. Such Club-purchased membership shall be eligible for resale, as the Board shall direct.

1.4. If an Equity Membership is retired during the calendar year, the Member will not be reimbursed for any dues paid for that year and shall be responsible for the payment of dues until the expiration of the calendar year, or until the membership is repurchased, whichever is first to occur.

Section 2: Transfer Upon Death

Upon the death of a Member, the deceased Member's spouse shall have the right to have the membership transferred to him or her without further membership contribution. If the surviving spouse does not elect to have the membership transferred within three months of the date of the Member's death, or if there is no surviving spouse, then the membership shall be treated as though the Member has resigned under Section 1 of this Article, except that the obligation for further dues payment shall not apply.

Section 3: Transfer Upon Divorce

In the event of a divorce between married Members holding an Equity Membership in joint names, the Equity Membership shall be transferred to the Member awarded the membership in the divorce decree or in the property settlement agreement.

Article IX: Discipline

Section 1: General

Any Member, immediate family member, or guest who violates the Club Bylaw or Club Rules or whose conduct, actions, or attire are deemed improper or likely to endanger the welfare, safety, harmony, or good reputation of the Club or its Members, may be reprimanded, fined, suspended, or expelled from the Club by action of the Board of Governors. The Board of Governors shall be the sole judge of what constitutes improper conduct or conduct likely to endanger the welfare, safety, harmony, or good reputation of the Club or its Members.

Section 2: Minor Infractions

Any Member, immediate family member, or guest who violates Section 1 of this Article may be reprimanded or fined not more than $100 by the Board, or the President, on behalf of the Club without further notice or hearing, except the reprimanded or fined person shall have the right to appeal such penalty to the Board within 30 days following written notice of such penalty. Thereupon the Board shall give the person an opportunity to appear before the Board and protest such reprimand or fine. Following the appeal, the Board shall rescind such reprimand or fine or affirm or modify such reprimand or fine and shall have the right to impose a lesser or greater penalty (including suspension).

Section 3: Major Infractions

3.1. Any Member, immediate family member, or guest of a Member who violates Section 1 of Article IX who shall be subject to a fine in excess of $100 or suspension or expulsion shall be given at least 21 days' written notice of the infraction or violation, the range of possible penalties, and the time and place where the Board will decide the penalty, if any, to be imposed. The person shall have the right to appear and be heard before the Board, with counsel and witnesses, if desired. The decision of the Board shall be delivered promptly (in writing) to the person charged.

3.2. The Board shall have the power to suspend a Member, immediate family member, or guest for a period of up to one year, during which period the person shall have no privileges at the Club, including the right to be a guest, but the Member shall have the responsibility to pay dues during such period. The suspension of a Member shall not apply to the Member's immediate family. The suspension of an immediate family member or guest shall apply only to the immediate family member or guest.

3.3. The Board may, by a two-thirds vote of the Members, expel a Member and revoke the Equity Membership under this Section 3. Upon revocation of the membership, the Member shall be deemed to have resigned and such resignation shall be handled in accordance with Article VIII hereof.

3.4. If the membership is in the joint names of husband and wife, the suspension of one spouse shall not affect the right to the use of the Club facilities by the other spouse, but the suspended Member shall have no right to use the Club's facilities as a guest of a Member.

Article X: Bylaw Definitions

Terms used in these Bylaws are defined as follows:

A. "Member" refers to the person or persons referred to on the membership application of the Club.
B. "Board" refers to the Board of Governors.
C. "Good standing" refers to the status of a Member who has not resigned, been terminated, or placed under suspension for disciplinary reasons or failure to meet financial obligations to the Club.
D. "Equity Membership Contribution" refers to the amount paid or to be paid for the purchase of an Equity Membership in a particular membership category, but excludes Initiation Fees.
E. "Significant other" refers to a person who is domiciled with and maintains a continuing relationship with an unmarried or divorced Member.

F. "Conflict Between Bylaws and Articles of Incorporation" means that in any conflict between these Bylaws and the Articles of Incorporation of the Club, the latter shall prevail.

Article XI: General
Section 1: Amendments
1.1. These Bylaws may be altered, amended, repealed, or new bylaws adopted by a majority vote of the Members of the Board of Governors, and a majority of the weighted votes cast by the Members voting.

Members may submit a petition to the Board signed by not less than 100 Members setting forth the requested changes in the Bylaws. Upon validation of signatures, the Board shall cause a ballot to be sent to the Membership within 15 days of verifying the signatures and such vote shall be completed within 60 days following the mailing of the ballots. A majority of the weighted votes cast by the Members voting shall effectuate the amendment.

Section 2: Dissolution
In the event of dissolution of the Club, all of the property and assets of the Club, after payment of all just debts and liabilities, shall be distributed to the Members in proportion to the amount of the Equity Membership Contribution then in effect for each Equity Membership category.

Section 3: Indemnification
Members of the Board of Governors, Club officers, and appointed committee members shall be indemnified and held harmless from and against any claims or threats of claim, whether civil, criminal, administrative, or investigative, by reason of being a Governor, officer, or committee member of the Club. Such person shall be indemnified against judgments, fines, or amounts paid in settlement, together with reasonable expenses (including attorney fees) incurred in connection with claims indemnified against. A judicial finding of actual fraud or willful misconduct shall preclude indemnification.

Index

Here are some other books on similar topics from Pineapple Press. For a complete catalog, write to Pineapple Press, P.O. Box 3889, Sarasota, Florida 34230-3889, or call (800) 746-3275. Or visit our website at www.pineapplepress.com.

The Business of Special Events by Harry A. Freedman and Karen Feldman. Successful nonprofit managers know that to raise money for their cause they must approach fundraising as if it were a for-profit business. This how-to covers every aspect of producing profitable special events, from sidewalk sales to glamorous galas. ISBN 1-56164-141-3 (pb)

Games for Fundraising by William N. Czuckrey. Who doesn't love a fair? The barker's cry, "Step right up, ladies and gentlemen!," the sound of hoops clattering over pegs and balls hitting their targets, the colorful booths, the mysterious fortune-tellers—all contribute to the excitement and fun of trying your luck or skill to win a prize. And it all adds up to substantial profits for the sponsoring organization. For anyone who is faced with the challenge of creating an exciting special event to raise funds with games, this book offers a selection of games sure to delight all ages, complete with step-by-step instructions. ISBN 1-56164-074-3 (pb)

Keep the Money Coming Revised Edition by Christine Graham. Every nonprofit organization needs to find a reliable way to fund the budget—every year. This book offers nonprofit organizations the basic skills for annual fundraising, with an underlying emphasis on strategy and capacity-building—the keys to long-term financial security. You will find charts, checklists, and guidelines to simplify the process and lead you to success. You will find powerful tools, sage advice, and proven methods to help you raise the money your organization needs every year. ISBN 1-56164-227-4 (pb)

Organizing Special Events and Conferences Revised Edition by Darcy C. Devney. Here is help for anyone who has to produce a public event—from a church social or school fundraiser to a national conference. This comprehensive and practical handbook is the first to reveal all the tricks and techniques of the professional event organizer. An indispensable guide for volunteers and paid staff alike, packed with step-by-step instructions, checklists, and schedules. Helpful hints and anecdotes from professionals and volunteers working at all types of organizations supplement the author's clear organization and lively presentation. Updated to include website information and e-mail addresses for dozens of fundraising associations, catalogs and directories, and publications. ISBN 1-56164-217-7 (pb)

A Primer on Nonprofit PR: If Charity Begins at Home . . . by Kathleen A. Neal. Kathleen Neal shows how public relations can be used creatively and effectively for nonprofit organizations. This book is chock full of ideas and strategies for applying solid PR techniques to the nonprofit, often accompanied by personal accounts of successful (and not so successful) PR efforts described with insight and a wry sense of humor. Plan a fundraising event, deal with a crisis, defuse a tense situation, develop a relationship with the media, and all the while promote your organization, keeping its mission in the eye of the public. Let this book be your how-to manual for a successful public relations program. ISBN 1-56164-229-0 (pb)